Doug Moran

Jerry Bertney

IPSWICH TOWN

Champions 1961/62

Best Wishes

Andy Nelson

Best Wishes

Jrayton

Best Wish.

IPSWICH TOWN

Champions 1961/62

MARTIN BROOKS

Foreword by Ray Crawford

The
History
Press

First published 2011

The History Press
The Mill, Brimscombe Port
Stroud, Gloucestershire, GL5 2QG
www.thehistorypress.co.uk

British Library Cataloguing in Publication Data.
A catalogue record for this book is available from the British
Library.

ISBN 978 0 7524 5890 8

Typesetting and origination by The History Press
Printed in Malta.

Contents

Acknowledgements

Thank you to Dave Kindred and Dave Cull for the supply of photographs and illustrations. Thank you to Paulene for her support and motivation. Thank you to Ray Crawford, Doug Moran, Larry Carberry and Jimmy Leadbetter for their time and assistance. Finally, thank you to Sir Alf Ramsey and all of the team of 1961/62 season for making Ipswich Town an exceptional football club.

Every effort has been made to trace the copyright holders of illustrations. If any infringement has taken place, then please inform the publishers and this will be rectified in future editions of the book.

Foreword
by Ray Crawford

Although I was born in Portsmouth and played my first twenty Football League Division One games for them, it was Ipswich Town where I made my name in football. I signed for the Town in the office of Fulham Football Club just before a game in which Fulham beat Ipswich 3–2.

During my ten years at the club I played under four managers – Sir Alf Ramsey, Sir Bobby Robson, Jackie Milburn and Bill McGarry – winning two Division Two titles and that great Division One championship in the 1961/62 season, when I scored 33 goals and my good mate Ted Phillips 28. We were known as 'the terrible twins'. I played 354 games and scored 228 goals for the Town and being part of that great team, I'm sure, helped to give me the chance to become an England international player.

In my first two years at Ipswich we didn't do too much, but the great Alf Ramsey was putting together a team that would make the country realise that Ipswich was not just a sleepy Suffolk market town with a small football club. In 1960/61 we won the Division Two title and Alf had got his team in place:

Roy Bailey

Larry Carberry   Andy Nelson   Ken Malcolm
(John Compton)

John Elsworthy   Reg Pickett
(Bill Baxter)

Roy Stephenson   Jimmy Leadbetter

Ted Phillips   Ray Crawford   Doug Moran

When Reg Pickett was injured, Bill Baxter came in for him and stayed in the team, John Compton came in to replace Ken Malcolm who was injured and also stayed. This was the team that went on to play in Division One – today's Premier League. Everyone said we would have no chance and come straight back down. How wrong they were. We started slowly, but as the season progressed we more than held our own. When clubs came to Portman Road, they could not believe what we had; our club dressing room was an old cricket pavilion with a wooden floor and no heating. There was one communal bath and a shower, and the toilets were at the back without any lights! At half time some of the lads would have a crafty fag there.

I'm sure Alf knew, but didn't say anything. Despite all this we had one of the best pitches in the league and we played to a formation that took other clubs two seasons to figure out. I remember Bobby Charlton saying 'I can't believe we lost 4–1 when we had 80 per cent of the game!' I also remember Alf telling us, 'the ball will get there faster than the man, so pass the ball quickly, short or long, it's up to you.' He worked on players' weaknesses and left the good things alone.

Ted and I just hit it off; we never had to work at our partnership. Ted would thunder in shots from outside the box, while I took them inside. We both owed a lot to Roy Stephenson and Jimmy Leadbetter who Alf got to drop deep in our half to receive the ball, but both could cross the ball into the box as well; most of all though, it was team effort that got Ipswich Town the results they deserved.

Alf would give a team talk on a Friday after training, going into great detail about the opposition; then on match days he would just tell us to enjoy ourselves. At half time he would make adjustments if he needed to. After the game it was, 'well done, you played well; see you at 10 a.m. on Tuesday,' but if you didn't it would be 'see you on Monday at 10 a.m. sharp!' There was no shouting or bawling at his players. The following Thursday Alf would go round each player going through the previous game. His memory was great and he pulled no punches if need be. It was as a result of his success at Ipswich that Alf Ramsey got the job as manager of England and using the same formation, won the World Cup. He was also quite rightly made Sir Alf Ramsey.

Ipswich supporters have been given some good times, and like most clubs they've seen bad times in football, but winning the league title in my mind is the best way to repay those fans. In this book you will relive all the great moments of the games during the 1961/62 season, how players had good or bad games and how the team got their results.

Introduction

I began watching Ipswich Town in April 1971, when I was ten years old. I don't recall when I first learned that what was now my team had once lifted the biggest prize in English football, the First Division Championship, but I do know that when I found out I was staggered. Throughout my first dozen years as a supporter of the Town, the First Division Championship was like the Holy Grail. Year after year Bobby Robson's team came so tantalisingly close to grasping that prize, yet they always contrived to throw the opportunity away some time during late April. Winning it seemed like an impossible dream, but the fact was the club had already achieved this feat. This meant Ipswich Town really were as good as Liverpool or Arsenal or Leeds United, those 'big' teams who were known for winning the important trophies. How I wished that I had been a particularly precocious child who had started attending Portman Road soon after my first birthday, or that I had been born ten years earlier.

Today, Town winning the Premier League (what a daft name for League Division One that is) seems as likely as my playing for them. But don't imagine that the Premier League is really any different to the old Division One Championship of 1961. Truthfully, the Premier League is the First Division with a brand name and the addition of several hundreds of millions of pounds, most of it in the pockets of owners, agents, managers and players. Despite the efforts of some record books and television channels, there was no line to be drawn after 1992 when the top division 'broke away'. Now, as then, there are four divisions of professional football in England comprising ninety-two teams in total. Ipswich winning the Football League in 1962 was therefore exactly the same achievement as winning the Premier League today; everything is relative.

In 2001 Town finished fifth in the Premier League, the season after having been promoted. Football pundits were astonished, so much so that they voted Ipswich's George Burley Manager of the Season, an unprecedented move from a bunch of people who more often than not simply give the award to the manager of the champions, but then again perhaps they too had become bored with Manchester United? Because everyone seems to believe that the Premier League is of such a fabulously high standard it was as if the modern team, or squad as it now was, had matched the achievement of the 1961/62 Championship-winning side. But, whereas in 2001 Ipswich Town were the fifth best team in the country after a meagre 38 matches, the 1962 team were the very best after 42 games and they remain the only team ever to have been promoted to the top division to have then won the League Championship at their very first attempt. It is difficult to imagine any team ever repeating this feat, but more significantly perhaps it was equally as difficult for anyone to imagine at the time that any club, particularly one like Ipswich Town, would perform this triumph. If the same thing were to happen today then a club such as Doncaster Rovers or Plymouth Argyle or even Colchester United would win what is now called the Championship and then take the Premier League title the following season.

The main part of this book is a match-by-match and month-by-month account of the 1961/62 season for Ipswich Town, with reports based on the facts gleaned from the sports pages of the local and national papers at the time. At the end of each month I attempt to set the football in the context of what was going on in the wider world. I begin, however, with a short analysis of how that famous Championship win came about, drawing on references from contemporary books and commentaries. There is no 'in-depth' analysis because football really is a simple game and a few words are generally all that is needed. My aim is to provide a small insight into the success of Ipswich Town that season, to relive how they won the Championship and as First Division 'virgins' achieved something never done before or since in well over a century of English professional football.

1   1961/62 & All That

I t is stating the obvious, but Britain in 1961 was very different to the Britain of today. All the towns and cities were in the same place (except Milton Keynes which wasn't built yet – what happy days for Wimbledon fans) and postboxes were still red, but that was about it. Most people didn't own a car and didn't own their own home; the Beatles were unheard of; man had not landed on (or been anywhere near) the moon; our currency was still firmly pounds, shillings and pence; Britain was not in the European Economic Community, etcetera, etcetera, etcetera. A great deal of change occurred in the 1960s, but in 1962 the 1950s were barely over and the Sixties had not begun to swing, if they ever did in Ipswich. As the poet Philip Larkin told us, this was the period between the end of the *Lady Chatterley* ban and the release of the Beatles' first LP – before 'sexual intercourse began'.

As far as professional football in England was concerned, the 1961/62 season *was* the beginning of a new era after one of the most important changes to the professional game ever seen in Britain, the abolition of the maximum wage. Back in 1961 this change was known as the 'New Deal' and it had come about after the Professional Footballers' Association, then led by Jimmy Hill of Fulham, had voted to strike, although in practice they eventually did not do so. This was the season that Johnny Haynes became the first player in England to earn £100 per week, but at Ipswich the wages were a quarter or a fifth of that amount.

The fact that the first season of the 'New Deal' should coincide with Ipswich Town winning the Football League First Division Championship at their first attempt was not without irony. Looking back we might think that the abolition of the maximum wage was the beginning of wages spiralling out of control, which has led to the situation where huge percentages of most clubs' turnovers are consumed by their players' wages and many sides teeter on the brink of financial ruin. But this does not seem to have been a concern shown by many club owners at the time. In the official *FA Yearbook* for 1962/63 Alan Hardaker, the secretary of the Football Association, wrote, 'So far as the actual wages paid are concerned, economics will solve that problem very quickly, but every player must realise that there is a limit to what he can take out of the game now if there is to be any game left for the players ten years hence.'

Much as today, the 'big' clubs were happy to pay the highest wages and indeed logic says that those clubs that are either able, or at least willing, to pay the highest wages, have an advantage as they should be able to capture the best players by giving them greater rewards than they would earn elsewhere. What English clubs were afraid of then was not losing players to their domestic rivals but to European clubs. Denis Law, Jimmy Greaves and John Charles had all joined Italian clubs for big fees and big salaries in the late 1950s and early 1960s but the abolition of the maximum wage put a stop to this exodus with Law and Greaves both returning to England fairly soon afterwards. In his book *My Fight for Football*, published in 1963, the then Burnley chairman Bob Lord expounded this view; 'Pay top price for what you want, provided, of course, the quality's there and you are satisfied you are getting value for money.'

Previously clubs could try to 'buy success' through the transfer market, but theoretically at least, no club could offer a player any greater financial incentive to play for them than another. The irony was therefore that Ipswich – the club with probably the least financial strength in the First Division – should win the Championship at their very first attempt in the very season when money was thought to have become the most important feature of the game. It may not be a coincidence however, that after Ipswich's success it would take until 1972 before another club outside Manchester, Liverpool or London would win the First Division Championship. Indeed, coming right up to date, in the forty-nine seasons since 1962 the Championship (or Premier League as it is now known) has been won by a club outside of Manchester, Liverpool or London just five times (Derby twice, Nottingham Forest, Aston Villa and Blackburn). So much for having a competitive league in England.

2   How Could It Have Happened?

For Ipswich Town to win the First Division Championship at their very first attempt was incredible. All the pundits had expected Town to be relegated, or at least struggle to stay in Division One – no one gave them any hope whatsoever of winning the title. Jimmy Greaves and Norman Giller in their book *The Sixties Revisited* had this to say, 'If there is such a thing as a miracle in football, then this was exactly what Alf Ramsey was performing at Ipswich.' In the *Topical Times Football Book* for 1963 a piece attributed to Jimmy Leadbetter says that at the start of the season the question was not which two clubs would be relegated but rather, 'Who goes down with Ipswich?', so certain was everyone that Ipswich would be unable to compete in the top flight of English football. David Coleman in the *BBC TV Sportsview Soccer Book* for 1962 perhaps summed up the dismissive attitude to Town when he wrote, 'Soccer laughed good naturedly at the thought of Ipswich being in Division One.'

Unfortunately, the shock of Ipswich's title win and their triumph over the clubs more beloved of the London-based press did result in some pretty terrible and lazy commentaries and articles being written.

With victory came the opportunity to parade the championship trophy around the town on an open-topped bus, supplied by the Eastern National Omnibus Company. The Royal Marine Band from HMS Ganges at nearby Shotley supplied the music. It is a great pity that the same trophy is now presented for merely winning the Second Division.

So how could everyone have been so wrong? What was the quality that Ipswich Town had that everyone had failed to see? Even the press, never usually short of an angle or two, were in some cases a bit stumped; in the *Observer* Tony Pawson described Town as a 'fascinating enigma' and wrote, 'No one outside Suffolk is quite able to believe in or explain their persistent success.' When I asked Jimmy Leadbetter what was the secret of Town's success in the 1961/62 season he had this to say, 'No secret. May be Alf had a secret but he never told us!'

3 Tactics

The commonly held view is that Alf Ramsey outwitted the whole division by developing a new tactic, much as he apparently did in creating his England team of wingless wonders that won the World Cup in 1966. Alf Ramsey was without any doubt tactically astute, but it could be that the winning tactic for Ipswich came about by chance as much as by any cunning plan devised by Mr Ramsey. This was certainly the view of Doug Moran who said this to me about the deep-lying wingers, 'He [Mr Ramsey] did not pre-plan that. He did that because you [Jimmy Leadbetter] preferred playing that way and Roy Stephenson too.' It was certainly the case that Alf Ramsey had assessed the strengths and abilities of the players he had at his disposal and he had created a system to make the most of their attributes.

Ipswich's special tactic or formation is now well known. At the time, the common formation for most League sides was 3-2-5, with teams having two wingers who pushed forward to get behind the full-backs and deliver crosses into the penalty box. What Ipswich did was to keep their wingers, Jimmy Leadbetter and Roy Stephenson, in deep positions. This somewhat flummoxed the opposition full-backs who were detailed to mark the wingers but now found they had to advance up the pitch to do so. This created large spaces behind them into which Stephenson and Leadbetter could place accurate long passes for Ray Crawford, Doug Moran and Ted Phillips to run onto. Many writers and commentators have highlighted the importance of Jimmy Leadbetter in the effective operation of this 'tactic'. In Dave Bowler's 1998 biography of Sir Alf Ramsey entitled *Winning isn't Everything* . . . he refers to 'Ipswich's Leadbetter formation' and says Jimmy Leadbetter became the playmaker of the team describing him thus, 'Intelligent and a good passer of the ball, but with the pace of an injured snail.' While stating the importance of Jimmy Leadbetter to the team, however, when he asks the question of who was the greatest player in the team, the answer he gives is 'The surprise formation. . .'.

Again, in Jimmy Greaves' and Norman Giller's *The Sixties Revisited*, they describe the formation as the forerunner of Alf Ramsey's 'revolutionary 4-3-3 England tactics. They add, 'Leadbetter . . . paralysed defenders with cunning running from a position alongside constructive midfield marshal Doug Moran. Many teams . . . tried to treat him [Leadbetter] like a conventional outside left, and defenders were drawn yards out of position as they tried to track his movements off the ball.'

The success of the tactic was borne out by Phillips' and Crawford's scoring figures of 28 and 33 goals respectively out of a total of 93 league goals scored by Town in the course of the Championship-winning season. Doug Moran was the third highest league goal scorer for the club with 14 and only

The First Division Champions 1961/62. Back row: John Compton, Billy Baxter, Andy Nelson, Roy Bailey, John Elsworthy and Larry Carberry. Front row: Roy Stephenson, Ray Crawford, Ted Phillips, Doug Moran and Jimmy Leadbetter.

three other players scored league goals, two of whom were the 'wingers' themselves, Roy Stephenson scoring 7 and Jimmy Leadbetter 8.

While the tactic of having the withdrawn wingers doubtless played a big part in Town's success it is not true to say, however, that this tactic had never been seen before and therefore that Town had ambushed Division One due to groundbreaking originality. In his 1970 biography of Alf Ramsey, *Anatomy of a Football Manager*, Max Marquis describes the tactic as being adapted from the Brazilians who had used a 4-2-4 formation and says, 'West Ham . . . were also using the formation . . . with initial success.'

4 'The Machine'

The idea that 'tactics' won Town the championship might suggest a simple victory of brain over brawn but this was far from the truth. In his 1968 book *The Football Man*, sports writer for the *Observer*, Arthur Hopcraft, described Ipswich's progress thus:

> Week by week in the seasons 1960–62 other teams' supporters watched the canny, lacklustre Ipswich stun more glamorous sides with a crushing, overall solidity of method. There were two big strikers up at the front to bang in the goals, never prettily, and behind them the machine pounded diligently and expertly. Perhaps there has never been a duller Championship side, and its success was the more commendable for that.

Hopcraft's description at first sounds critical, in the same way that twenty-five years later Fleet Street football writers would decry Wimbledon's aggressive, utilitarian 'long ball' style. But Hopcraft acknowledges that here was a highly efficient team at work, a 'machine' as he calls it and he clearly believed that despite being dull, the promotion of a team ethic above individual talent was worthy of praise. Indeed, there was no possibility of describing Town as a one-man, two-man or even three-man team; every single one of the eleven had an equal part to play.

Hopcraft's reference to there never having been a duller Championship side is given some credence by the words of Alf Ramsey himself who admitted that the first consideration for his team was having a solid defence. Dave Bowler quotes Alf Ramsey as saying, 'We believe in first, a concentrated, well organised defence in which every man must know how he is expected to play in relation to his team-mates. And second we believe in striking quickly from defence.' Some measure of Ipswich's defensive prowess is again referred to in Dave Bowler's book when he quotes England full-back Ray Wilson talking about an England match versus Argentina, 'It was like playing Ipswich – we had the ball for 85 minutes and lost 1–0.'

As much as Ipswich concentrated on a strong defence, however, they still managed to score 93 goals and let in 67, which by modern standards is a lot of goals scored and, for a table-topping team, a hell of a lot conceded too. The priorities described by Alf Ramsey would classify Town as having a 'counter-attacking' style if translated to the modern game and probably 'direct' or even 'long-ball' to boot. Ramsey considered that when coming out of defence the ball should be at the other end of the field within three or four passes and that by the time of the final pass, a strike on goal should be possible. His belief was that the opposition were at their most vulnerable just when their own attacking move had broken down, and that the fewer passes your own team made in getting the ball forward, the fewer opportunities there were for your own play to break down and for possession to be lost to the opposition again. Once again, this was the thinking of exponents of the 'long-ball' game such as Stan Cullis at Wolverhampton Wanderers in the 1950s and, later on, the likes of Graham Taylor at Watford in the late 1970s and obviously Dave Bassett at Wimbledon in the 1980s.

Of course today the 'long-ball' style of football is unpopular among many fans and commentators on the game who see it as ugly and lacking skill. But even if Ipswich did use the long ball, which should probably be more accurately described as the 'long pass', their play was certainly not unattractive. James Wilson, columnist for the *Sunday Times* reported on Ipswich in March 1962 thus, 'The ball always worked, never thumped haphazardly out of defence, intelligent taking of position in midfield, a pleasing economy of effort – there are many similar reminders of the golden days of push and run.' Alf Ramsey had of course been a member of the Tottenham Hotspur Championship-winning team of 1950/51, which was famed for its 'push and run' style of play.

The final word in this section goes to David Coleman in his article in the *BBC TV Sportsview Soccer Book* for 1962. Coleman wrote of Ipswich, 'They have proved their worth, not by flukes or bludgeon, but by pure football played in a simple, direct way that leads to goals and movements of beauty.'

5   Alf Ramsey

The Ipswich Town side of 1961/62 had no real stars, being a collection of unheard-of players and those released by other clubs. At the centre of this seemingly motley collection was one man; the manager Alf Ramsey, who had been an England international player and was truly a star, destined within five years to guide the England team to their only success, aside from winning the now-defunct Home International Championship, that is. There is no doubt at all that Alf Ramsey was central to Town's Championship win. In the 1962 *Caxton Football Annual* John Cobbold, the chairman at the time, wrote, 'The credit for this success lies squarely on the shoulders of Alf Ramsey. He has the natural ability to produce the best from his players, and to blend them into a team.'

To get a full picture of Alf Ramsey it is best to read one of his biographies such as Max Marquis's *Anatomy of a Football Manager* written in 1970 or the later (1998) work by Dave Bowler entitled *Winning isn't Everything . . . a Biography of Sir Alf Ramsey*. The latter in particular makes many references to Ramsey's time as Ipswich's manager and the Championship win of 1962.

But the reason for Ramsey's success can surely be traced back to a handful of qualities that he possessed, the combination of which made him special. In the previous section reference was made to Ramsey's tactical awareness and this stemmed from his near obsession with the game of football to the extent that he thought and talked about little else. Doug Moran had this to say about Ramsey, 'I think he lived for football. I remember coming back from games on the train. You used to avoid him. You'd run along the corridor.' Larry Carberry, also talking about the train journeys back from away matches added, 'You used to have what, eight or ten compartments. He'd start talking in this one and he'd bore us all and then we'd change the conversation – "Did you see that film last night?" – and he'd get up and walk next door.'

Alf Ramsey had a phenomenal capacity to remember details about games and this helped him to both coach his players and formulate his team. Larry Carberry said of Ramsey's memory, 'Every mistake we made in a match or every good thing we did he could point it out to us, he had it all up here and he'd say why did you do this? He could tell you a week later and tell you every mistake you made in a match, it was uncanny.'

Ramsey's wonderful memory for each player's shortcomings and attributes must have helped him enormously in assembling this team, which was clearly greater than the sum of its parts. This was why Ramsey was confident that the team with which he had won the Second Division in 1961 would be good enough, with the single addition of Doug Moran, to compete in the First Division. In the *All Stars Football Book* of 1962 Ray Crawford wrote, 'He [Ramsey] tells us . . . how we can play to the maximum of our strength.

Ipswich Town Football Club, Limited.

Portman Road Ground, Ipswich.

PRACTICE MATCH

TUESDAY, AUGUST 8th, 1961

BLUES *v.* REDS

Kick-off 6.30 p.m.

REDS

1—HALL

| 2—BRYANTON | | 3—STIFF |

| 4—PICKETT | 5—LAUREL | 6—COMPTON |

7—STEPHENSON 8—MORAN 9—CRAWFORD 10—PHILLIPS 11—LEADBETTER

Referee: *Linesmen:*
Mr. J. H. CHAMBERLAIN R. A. DRIVER and D. V. BROOK

11—OWEN   10—REES   9—MILLWARD   8—CURTIS   7—TREACY

6—ELSWORTHY   5—NELSON   4—BAXTER

3—MALCOLM   2—CARBERRY

1—BAILEY

BLUES

Players to be introduced at half time:—THROWER, THOMPSON, KEARNEY, McKAY

FORTHCOMING ATTRACTIONS

August 19th v. SHREWSBURY TOWN (Combination) Kick-off 3.0 p.m.

August 26th v. MANCHESTER CITY (League) Kick-off 3.0 p.m.

August 29th v. BURNLEY (League) Kick-off 7.30 p.m.

September 2nd v. MANSFIELD TOWN (Combination) Kick-off 3.0 p.m.

OFFICIAL PROGRAMME, 1d.

E.A.D.T., IPSWICH

The team sheet from a pre-season practice match shows that Alf Ramsey pitched his first choice forwards in the 'Reds' against his first choice backs in the 'Blues'. Sadly for Ken Malcolm an early season injury would mean that he was only to feature in the first three games of the season with his place being taken by John Compton for the remaining thirty-nine.

Nobody claims we have the greatest individual players in the league, but we reckon our team play is second to none.' It is interesting to see how many of Town's team were playing in different positions to those in which they originally set out on their footballing careers. Both Jimmy Leadbetter and Roy Stephenson had been inside forwards, but had been converted to wide players by Ramsey. Similarly John Compton had moved from wing-half to full-back, Bill Baxter from centre-half to wing-half and Andy Nelson, from left-half to centre-half. When I spoke with Larry Carberry he said of Ramsey, 'I always say that Alf got the best out of me and I think he got the best out of most of us.'

Ramsey's ability to evaluate each of his player's strengths dovetailed perfectly with his belief in team play and eschewing too much individuality in players. This would later show itself in his selections for the 1966 World

Architect of the Championship win, Alf Ramsey, pictured in his office at Portman Road. He is seen in a particularly handsome double-breasted club blazer which sports the club crest on the breast pocket. Forget replica shirts, club blazers are sure to be the must-have accessory for Town fans from now on.

Cup when he would leave Jimmy Greaves out of his team. In the *Topical Times Football Book* for 1962 a piece attributed to Jimmy Leadbetter tells us, 'He [Ramsey] . . . insists there are no stars at Ipswich. A team is eleven players. No one is any better than anyone else. Because of this outlook every player at Ipswich is playing for the other. All are prepared to help out. Forwards go back and help in defence.' At a time when Dutch international football had yet to get going at all, it seems Ipswich Town had already embraced 'Total Football'!

The combination of his knowledge and insight, with his belief in the team ethic inspired huge loyalty from his players and Ramsey reciprocated in spades. In his biography of Alf Ramsey Max Marquis wrote, 'The players had enormous respect for him, as all his players always have. When he talked football to them, they knew he was talking practical sense . . . He also radiated faith in them to which they naturally responded.' Dave Bowler wrote of Ramsey in his biography of the man, 'Alf's greatest gift to the Ipswich squad was team spirit . . . Alf was . . . an exceptional man-manager.'

Ramsey's loyalty to his players is perhaps shown by the fact that he only signed one new player (Doug Moran) for the 1961/62 season despite the popular opinion that the players he had were not good enough for Division One. A wonderful illustration of his loyalty was in his treatment of Ted Phillips. During the middle part of the season Phillips was out of form; he was barracked by sections of the Portman Road crowd, and the *East Anglian Daily Times* sports editor, Alan Everitt, was extremely critical of him too. But Phillips played on throughout, the only two games he missed being through injury. In the *BBC TV Sportsview Soccer Book* of 1962 it describes how broadcaster John Arlott asked how long Ramsey would keep playing Phillips after three months of poor form; 'Another three months,' was Ramsey's terse reply.

Such resolute faith in his players resulted in great self-confidence among all the players. In his biography of Ramsey, Max Marquis states, 'The talent of Ramsey for making players believe in themselves was an absolutely essential part of Ipswich's First Division success.' In conversation with Larry Carberry, Jimmy Leadbetter and Doug Moran I was struck by their great admiration for Alf Ramsey. Doug Moran summed up his feelings in just seven heartfelt words, 'You always wanted to play for him.'

6 The Competition: Burnley & Tottenham Hotspur

Clearly Ipswich beat twenty-one other football clubs over forty-two games in order to win the Football League First Division Championship. However, at the start of the season most people expected the race for the Championship to be between just two clubs, Burnley (champions in 1960) and Tottenham Hotspur (the 1961 champions *and* FA Cup holders). For much of the season it appeared that there was only one team to beat; Burnley, for they led the table, often with a clutch of games in hand, from September to March.

Burnley had set out at the start of the season believing that they could emulate Tottenham Hotspur and win the league and cup double. In his book, *My Fight for Football*, published in 1963, Burnley's notorious chairman Bob Lord plainly says as much.

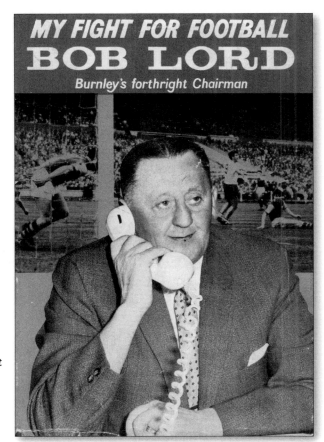

Town's main rivals in the title race were Burnley, another 'small town club' led by a charismatic chairman. But in Burnley's case their chairman, Bob Lord, was a local tradesman rather than a member of the aristocracy. The difference in their respective styles is illustrated perhaps by Bob Lord's evident need to put his views into print; his book was published in 1963. (Bob Lord, My Fight for Football, *published by S. Paul, 1963)*

Tottenham were by far the bigger of the two rivals having average crowds in excess of 45,000 whereas only one other club in Division One (Everton) could even claim average crowds of 40,000. This gave them the ability to spend much more heavily in the transfer market and indeed during the course of the 1961/62 season they paid £99,999 to AC Milan for the signature of Jimmy Greaves. Having been domestic 'double' winners the season before, Tottenham were desperate to impress in the European Cup. Phil Soar, in his *Official Illustrated History of Tottenham Hotspur 1882–1997* begins his section on their European Cup campaign with these words, 'No British club has ever entered the European Cup with more confidence than did Spurs on 13 September 1961.' Despite it being the first time they had played in European competition, Tottenham's optimism was justified as they reached the semi-final where they eventually lost to Benfica. They also prospered in the FA Cup, actually winning the trophy for the second year running, against the country's other top team, Burnley. Tottenham's cup runs must certainly have given them plenty to think about other than the league and this might have been a reason for their failure to match Ipswich in the race for the title. According to Phil Soar, 'Tottenham took their eye off the ball over the last few laps of the league race. Five crucial home points were dropped in the last six matches to be played at White Hart Lane and that was definitely not championship form.' What he doesn't say, however, is that two of those five points were lost at home to Ipswich, while another two were lost in the last home game of the season, by which time Tottenham could no longer win the Championship in any case. So Tottenham's challenge did not so much collapse in the run in as fade away gradually over the course of the season, until just Burnley and Ipswich were left in contention.

Burnley were possibly more disappointed not to win the league than Tottenham. Certainly they should have been because for six months they led the table, often by several points and with games in hand. Burnley could be said perhaps to have had fewer excuses for their failure than Tottenham because they had fewer games to play, not being involved in European competition. Nevertheless, Burnley did reach the FA Cup final like Tottenham, although also like Tottenham, but unlike Ipswich, they declined to enter the League Cup (at its inception, entry into the League Cup was optional and some of the bigger clubs did not bother to enter; it was not taken particularly seriously by many First Division clubs as is evidenced by the fact that the 1961/62 final was contested between Rochdale and Norwich City and Norwich City won). Over the course of the whole season the three rivals played the following numbers of competitive matches:

Ipswich Town:	42 league + 5 FA Cup + 5 League Cup	= 52 Games
Burnley:	42 league + 8 FA Cup	= 50 Games
Tottenham Hotspur:	42 league + 7 FA Cup + 8 European Cup	= 67 Games

In his book *My Fight for Football* Bob Lord devotes a whole chapter to Burnley's failure to win the league and FA Cup double in a chapter entitled 'My Nightmare'. In Bob Lord's assessment everything was going well for Burnley until 18 March when he developed appendicitis. 'Then the troubles of an over-taxed team began to arrive – injuries to players,' stated Lord, adding, 'In one important league game we lacked all three regular members of the half-back line, and so it went on.'

Lord rejected any claim that having been ahead and with games in hand Burnley threw the league title away. 'That is rubbish. Too many matches had to be played in too short a period. Eleven vital games in twenty-seven days, an average of one game every two and a half days. Each game filled with tension on brain, muscle and tendon . . . that is the explanation.'

Certainly Bob Lord made a fair point. Despite actually playing fewer competitive matches than Ipswich over the whole season, Burnley were placed in the unenviable position of having to play one-fifth of those games in the final month of a nine-month season. Of those ten league matches Burnley won just one and drew five, giving them a meagre seven points from the last twenty on offer. By contrast Ipswich were able to harvest fourteen points from their final ten matches, only six of which were played in April.

The diagram below shows how the Burnley and Ipswich teams each gathered their points across the course of the season.

In addition to playing club matches, many of Burnley's players were called upon to play in representative teams, with ten members of their senior side being international players at either full or under-23 level. Such was the number of international players in Burnley's team, they were permitted to call off games if they had to field an under-strength team. This created understandable problems for the team manager as postponed fixtures

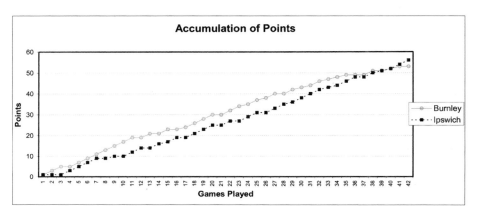

The most noticeable features in Burnley's record are their excellent start to the season, notwithstanding their 6–2 thrashing at Portman Road in only the fourth game, and their slowing return of points from about game thirty onwards. After Burnley's heavy defeat at Ipswich they had then embarked on a club record run of seven consecutive League victories.

inevitably created the possibility of fixture congestion later on, but on the other hand this made it possible for the team to go three weeks without playing. As an example, on 7 October Burnley postponed their game at home to Blackburn Rovers because of international call-ups. The following week Burnley's fixture was at West Ham United and despite international call-ups again they elected to play, but lost 2–1. The Blackburn game was eventually not played until 17 April and they lost that too, by 1–0. Perhaps they chose to postpone the wrong fixture, but that's easy to say in hindsight.

Despite the Burnley team's failure to lift a trophy, their captain Jimmy Adamson still made off with the Footballer of the Year accolade from the Football Writers' Association, perhaps due to his international efforts as assistant to the England manager, Walter Winterbottom, as much as his club achievements. Adamson was attributed with a piece in the 1962 *Caxton Football Annual* entitled 'How Burnley Lost the Double'. In this piece Adamson doesn't complain about fixture congestion but rather admits that in the first three-quarters of the season Burnley had the rub of the green, especially in the early games when, as he puts it, they 'seemed to score goals at will.' then however, 'a month or two before the season ended, our luck ran out in front of goal.' He goes onto to point out that they also suffered a spate of injuries at a crucial time when younger players had to be pressed into the team for high-pressure games. Burnley actually used nineteen players over the course of the season as opposed to Ipswich's record low of sixteen. Many of the youngsters such as Andy Lochhead and John Talbut, who only played odd games in 1961/62 season, became far more established in the team the following year however, so they were by no means without talent. But, the third reason he gives for Burnley's missing out on top placing in the league was, 'Ipswich's great run of victories on the last lap of the season. They undoubtedly deserved their success in the final reckoning.'

While Burnley and Tottenham were the two teams who started as favourites for the league title, and they finished in second and third place, there was one other club who came reasonably close, finishing just one point behind Tottenham with 51 points. This club was Everton, who had finished fifth the previous season, and are worth mentioning because they were destined to win the league championship the following season, 1962/63. Everton's form across the whole season was pretty good, and their home record of seventeen wins and just two defeats matched Town's as the best in the division; indeed it was better than Ipswich's if you consider that they scored six more goals and conceded seven fewer. Two things however, let Everton down in their 1961/62 campaign. First was their record of six defeats in the first ten games, including three consecutive losses immediately prior to their 5–2 home win over Ipswich on 16 September. Second was their away form, with only three victories away from Goodison Park, although they lost only one game more than Town. Overall they had the best defensive record in the league, conceding a total of 54 goals in the forty-two games.

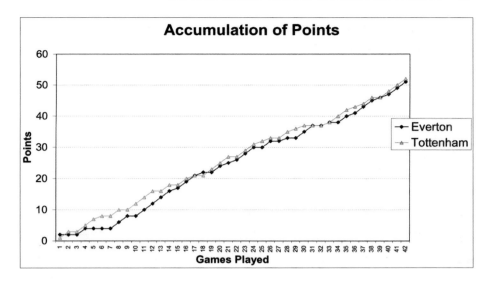

The diagram above shows the rate at which Tottenham and Everton gathered their points over the course of the league season.

Burnley and Tottenham probably should have done better, but they didn't, and that is the case with every 'fancied' side that doesn't win the league title every year. Ipswich Town would regrettably join the ranks of failed contenders many times over in later seasons under Bobby Robson, but in 1961/62 there is no question that over forty-two games they had what was needed to be champions. They had exactly what the other clubs did not have, simply the ability to keep going.

7 Going to the Match

Portman Road in 1961 was inevitably very different to the stadium that the present team plays in. Most noticeable would have been the terracing, it being a full thirty years before the imposition of 100 per cent seating and the loss of atmosphere that has engendered at so many games, along with the scandalous hike in admission prices.

Looking at the earlier history of the ground, a wooden stand on Portman Road had been constructed for the start of the 1936/37 season when Town first joined the Southern League, and the North Stand bank had been built up and roofed in 1936, then concrete terraces laid in 1954. The South Stand or 'Churchmans' had been built by the time Town joined the Football League in 1938. It wasn't until 1957 that a West Stand was built with a central section erected behind existing terracing; this was extended just a year later to fill the whole side of the ground. The 1959/60 season saw the erection of floodlight pylons at Portman Road and the lights were switched on by Lady Blanche Cobbold (the chairman's mum) at a friendly game versus Arsenal on Tuesday 16 February 1960. For the 1961/62 season the only changes to the ground were the laying of new concrete terracing in the North Stand and some additional turnstiles.

Also on Princes Street, and a landmark of sorts for supporters down the years, the Sporting Farmer pub (renamed the Drum & Monkey in 1990) was built for the Tolly Cobbold brewery during the course of the 1961/62 season.

In August 1961 the ground therefore consisted of two covered terraces behind each goal, a low wooden seated stand behind a terrace on the Portman Road side and a 'modern' seated stand with a terraced 'paddock' along the length of the ground's west side. The dressing rooms and offices were still housed in former Army huts in the south-west corner.

The streets around the ground were beginning to change in the early 1960s. On Princes Street the office block Shell Mex House (no. 153) was just being completed while neighbouring Fison House (now the Berkeley Business Centre) was also new. While these two new buildings had meant the loss of houses in Metz Street and Sedan Street, there were still many more residential streets close to the ground, though most would be demolished within a few years; streets set to disappear under Civic Drive included Perth Street and Castle Street, while the Greyfriars development would later swallow up Edgar Street, James Street and Portman Street among others.

Returning to Portman Road itself and the football ground, admission prices were as follows:

West Stand, North Stand and Churchman's terraces: 4s
Boys: 2s
East Terrace: 3s
Boys: 1s 6d
Seats: 6s 6d

Referring to concessions for young people as 'Boys' prices seems rather sexist nowadays doesn't it?

Programmes cost 4d (less than 2p in today's money) and consisted of twenty pages, including the front and back covers, in a roughly 10.5 cm x 13 cm (4.25 inches x 5.25 inches in 1961) format. The front cover was blue in colour with the words Ipswich Town Football Club above a black and white photo montage of Town supporters with a picture of Andy Nelson holding aloft the Second Division trophy in the centre. Beneath the photograph were the words 'Official Programme' and the price. The front cover remained exactly the same for every home game over the whole season.

The inside cover of the programme was an advertisement for Tolly Cobbold beers with the slogan 'after the match your local beers are best, Tolly Cobbold ales for quality'. Tolly Cobbold had a virtual monopoly on beer in the town back in the 1960s with the vast majority of pubs belonging to the Ipswich brewery. Few people would have drunk nationally available lager brands as these were rare and only in their infancy. For an appreciative beer drinker it must have been wonderful to be able to drink a beer pretty much exclusive to the locality wherever you went.

Page three carried the club directory with the names of the directors and club telephone number as well as details of the day's fixture – the

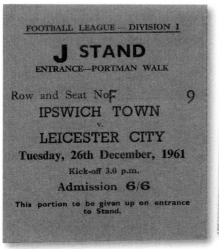

A selection of seat tickets from the West Stand. It is doubtful that there is anything you could buy today at a football ground for 32½ pence, the price of a seat in 1961/62. This simple type of coloured paper ticket was used at Portman Road up until the autumn of 1979.

kick-off time, opposition and competition, etc. – and there was also a list of forthcoming matches at Portman Road. Page four was a full-page advertisement for the Ipswich Co-op men's department, while page five was headed 'Secretary-Manager's Notes' and offered the thoughts of Alf Ramsey on recent games.

Page six carried two advertisements, one for J. & J. Edwards, a school outfitters in Tavern Street and, the other for the Norfolk & Suffolk Hospitals Contributors' Association under the banner 'Prepare for the unexpected . . .'. This offered various degrees of health insurance starting at 3*d* per week.

Page seven listed details of players' appearances and goalscorers as well as announcing the winner of the previous Lucky Programme Number competition and the half-time scoreboard. For midweek games an advertisement for the *East Anglian Daily Times* and *Evening Star* might replace the half-time scoreboard.

Page eight carried a full-page advert for the Ipswich Steam Laundry in nearby Alderman Road with the information that they were the launderers to the football club. Page nine displayed the latest league table as well as advertisements for the Odeon and Gaumont cinemas with details of which films were currently showing.

The centre pages, ten and eleven, displayed the team line-ups, laid out in the 2-3-5 formation longways across the two pages. At the top and bottom of the 'pitch' were advertisements for Footman's the department store (now Debenhams) and Croydon's the jewellers. The Footman's advert encouraged you to book a table in their restaurant where there were set menu lunches for 3s 6d, 4s 6d and 7s 6d, and afternoon tea for 3s 6d.

Page twelve introduced the day's visiting team with pen pictures of their players, while page thirteen consisted of advertisements for Grimwade's clothing store on the corner of Westgate Street and Cornhill and Churchman's Tipped cigarettes.

Page fourteen listed the first team and reserve fixtures and opposite on page fifteen there were adverts for Churchman's Tenners cigarettes and for Gould's butcher's shops at 29–31 St Margaret's Street and 14 Orford Street.

Page sixteen displayed a team photo at the start of the season but later on this was replaced by tables of players' appearances in Reserve and Border League fixtures.

Page seventeen consisted of an advertisement for Price's footwear shop which was on the corner of Lower Brook Street and Tacket Street, and an advertisement for British Railways. Fans travelling to away games by train could get discounts of at least 25 per cent if travelling in a party of eight or more. For the game at West Bromwich the fare on the train was 34s, while the return journey to Fulham cost 12s 6d plus Underground fares.

Page eighteen was given over to the Ipswich Town Supporters Club notes and an advertisement for Warner's heating engineers who, the advert tells us, provided the irrigation equipment for the Portman Road pitch.

There were three advertisements on the inside of the back cover of the programme; for Cubitt & Gotts the builders, the Green 'Un, which cost 3d, and Tyler & Son who sold electrical goods.

Finally, the back of the programme was a full-page advertisement for the Eastern Counties Building Society of 13 Queen St.

Away from home, programmes varied in price between 3d at Aston Villa, Bolton, Blackburn, Blackpool, West Bromwich, and Tottenham, and 6d at Chelsea (they've obviously always been expensive!), Arsenal, West Ham, Fulham and Manchester City. Like Ipswich, however, the other clubs,

Manchester United, Leicester, Nottingham Forest, Birmingham, Cardiff, Wolves, Sheffield United, Wednesday and Everton charged 4d for their programmes. No club saw fit to charge 5d, probably because that would have needed three coins rather than just one or two.

The programmes for all Ipswich Town's home games in the 1961/62 season looked like this, with a picture in the centre of Andy Nelson lifting the Second Division Championship trophy. The dominant colour of the cover was royal blue with the photographs being in black and white. Most clubs had unchanging front covers to their programmes over the course of the season. Only Manchester United and West Ham United featured action photographs that changed from match to match.

8   The Games

August 1961

Match No. 1
Saturday 19 August 1961
Venue: Burnden Park
Bolton Wanderers 0–0 Ipswich Town   Attendance: 16,708

This was Ipswich Town's 700th league game and their first ever meeting with Bolton Wanderers at Burnden Park, or anywhere else come to that. Alf Ramsey selected the team that had played in the pre-season game at Arsenal the previous Saturday and drawn 3–3. Doug Moran made his debut in a competitive match for Town, playing in the inside right position. Town had travelled up to Lancashire the day before the match and based themselves in

The programme from Ipswich Town's first ever Football League Division One game, played away to Bolton Wanderers at their Burnden Park ground on Saturday 19 August 1961. The final score was 0–0. The programme was printed in blue ink with splashes of green – with the pitch on the front cover naturally being green. It was very common in the 1961/62 season for clubs to depict an aerial view of their stadium on the front cover of their programme. Ipswich was one of only a handful of First Division clubs not to show even a glimpse of a stand on the front of their programme.

Ipswich Town club captain Andy Nelson, followed by goalkeeper Roy Bailey, leads the team out at Burnden Park on 19 August 1961. It looks like many spectators and the Lancashire Constabulary had expected rain that afternoon.

Manchester, staying over for the game at Burnley on the following Tuesday. Bolton had only escaped relegation from Division One by three points in 1961, but were defensively quite solid, having conceded just 29 goals at home which was only one more than the defending champions Tottenham had let in.

Bolton manager Bill Ridding selected the following side: Hopkinson; Hartle and Farrimond; Rimmer, Edwards and Wilkinson; Holden, Stevens, McAdams, Hill and Pilkington. Goalkeeper Edward Hopkinson and wingers Holden and Pilkington had all previously been selected for England while Hill had played for the under-23s.

The Town team was: Bailey; Malcolm and Carberry; Baxter, Elsworthy and Nelson; Leadbetter, Moran, Crawford, Phillips and Stephenson. Reg Pickett had travelled as twelfth man but was not required and of course there were no substitutes permitted during games back in 1961.

After weathering a storm of attacks in the first twenty minutes, during which Bolton created two good chances, Town began to take up more of the initiative and made some worthwhile attacks of their own. In the end they might have taken both points if only they had enjoyed some better finishing. Twice in the first half Jimmy Leadbetter shot over the bar with the goal open before him and Ray Crawford repeated the 'trick' in the second half. Half-back Billy Baxter seemed most likely to score, rather than any of the forwards as he had one shot blocked and forced a full-length save from keeper Edward Hopkinson who tipped the ball onto the post from another.

Baxter took on the role of attacking half-back while Elsworthy played deeper and brought the ball out of defence. Their performance, and that of captain Nelson in winning the aerial duels, prompted the headline in the *Evening Star* of 'Town half-backs dominate Bolton match'. The forward play was not by any means as effective and despite what the *Evening Star* referred to as some 'dazzling' runs from Stephenson, Crawford and Phillips, did not react quickly enough on the ball.

There was one scare for Town in the sixtieth minute when Bill McAdams had the ball in the net for Bolton, but this was disallowed for an earlier foul by Stevens on Andy Nelson.

Overall this was a most satisfactory result and on the strength of this first game it seemed that Town would have no difficulty in at least holding their own in the First Division. The referee was Mr F. Allott of Sheffield.

The full list of results in Division One on the opening day of the 1961/62 season was as follows:

Arsenal	2–2	Burnley
Birmingham City	2–1	Fulham
Blackburn Rovers	0–0	Cardiff City
Blackpool	1–2	Tottenham Hotspur
Bolton Wanderers	0–0	Ipswich Town
Chelsea	2–2	Nottingham Forest
Everton	2–0	Aston Villa
Manchester City	3–1	Leicester City
Sheffield United	2–1	Wolverhampton Wanderers
West Bromwich Albion	0–2	Sheffield Wednesday
West Ham United	1–1	Manchester United

At this early stage in the season Tottenham Hotspur were the clear favourites for the title, being double winners from the previous season. Burnley were also thought to be very strong contenders having been the Championship winners in 1960.

Match No. 2
Tuesday 22 August 1961
Venue: Turf Moor
Burnley 4–3 Ipswich Town   Attendance: 24,577

This game was another first ever meeting with a second Lancashire club – this time it was Burnley, who had won the League Championship themselves as recently as 1960. Burnley were to complete an unwanted but nevertheless admirable 'double' in the 1961/62 season by finishing as runners-up in the 1961/62 league campaign and also runners-up to Tottenham Hotspur in the FA Cup.

Burnley in the early 1960s might be compared to the Ipswich Town team of 1980/81 season except they had actually managed to win the league before, in 1960. In the 1960/61 season they had reached the semi-finals of both domestic cups and the quarter final of the European Cup and finished fourth in the league. At the start of the 1961/62 season all their players were aged twenty-four or under apart from Jimmy Adamson and Jimmy McIlroy who were both in their late twenties.

The Burnley manager was Harry Potts and he selected the following team: Blacklaw; Joyce and Elder; Adamson, Cummings and Miller; Connelly, McIlroy, Pointer, Robson and Harris.

Town kept the same side that had drawn at Bolton: Bailey; Carberry and Malcolm; Elsworthy, Nelson and Baxter; Leadbetter, Moran, Crawford, Phillips and Stephenson. The referee was Mr R.T.E. Langdale of Darlington.

This was truly a magnificent game played at a blistering pace. Burnley chairman Bob Lord said it was one of the best seen at Turf Moor in a very long time, while the *Evening Star* described it as a 'seven-goal masterpiece' under a headline of 'Ipswich go down with their colours flying high'.

As early as the fourth minute Ted Phillips tried the first of four powerful long-range drives, hitting a post with Adam Blacklaw motionless in the Burnley goal. Moran was unlucky not to follow up another with a goal but these efforts aside it was Burnley who battered Ipswich with a series of skilful and intense attacks. Town held out until the twenty-third minute when McIlroy found James Robson on the left who then put Ray Pointer in with just Bailey to beat, which he did. Burnley's lead lasted fifteen minutes until Ted Phillips crashed home the proverbial bullet header from a Leadbetter cross. Unfortunately for Phillips, only minutes later he lost possession in the midfield and quickly Gordon Harris had made it 2–1 before Town could regroup and defend.

The second half was only seven minutes old when Town once more levelled the scores. This time Crawford reached a high through-ball and hit it hard into the ground; the bounce was too much for Blacklaw in the Burnley goal and Moran was able to tap the ball back to Crawford who hooked it into the net.

On sixty-four minutes Burnley were ahead for the third time as Brian Miller headed in John Connelly's centre. Stephenson forced a save from Blacklaw before, on seventy-three minutes, Phillips shot on the turn from 18 yards and Alex Elder could only deflect the ball into the Burnley net. Sadly parity lasted only four minutes as Connelly crossed low and Carberry stuck out a boot; the ball ballooned into the air and Bailey could only palm it into the air again. As Bailey and Carberry left it to one another to clear, McIlroy seized on the confusion and skilfully placed the ball beyond the four Town defenders who had assembled on the goal line.

The *Evening Star* singled out Ted Phillips as having had the match of a lifetime after his four long-range shots and Moran was also said to have worked tirelessly in midfield. The Burnley full-backs Joyce and Elder had troubled Town by constantly joining attacks and taking every opportunity to shoot, but it almost seems unfair to mention these things in a game which must assume mythical status for, as the *Evening Star* put it, 'There were so many incidents that they cannot all be recorded.'

Although Town had lost this fixture Alf Ramsey was quoted as saying, 'It is the best performance I have seen from any Ipswich team since I have been connected with the club. It was a wonderful match in which the football rose to a very high standard.'

The other results from the second round of league fixtures were as follows:

21 August
| Blackpool | 2–1 | Blackburn Rovers |

22 August
| Nottingham Forest | 2–1 | Birmingham City |

23 August
Cardiff City	1–1	Sheffield United
Fulham	3–4	Manchester City
Leicester City	0–1	Arsenal
Manchester United	3–2	Chelsea
Sheffield Wednesday	4–2	Bolton Wanderers
Tottenham Hotspur	2–2	West Ham United
West Bromwich Albion	2–0	Everton

Match No. 3
Saturday 26 August 1961
Venue: Portman Road
Ipswich Town 2–4 Manchester City   Attendance: 21,473

Town's third match of the season was yet another first-ever meeting with yet another Lancashire club, this time the 1936/37 season champions Manchester City. Commentary on the second half of this match was broadcast live on BBC radio; Raymond Glendenning was the commentator. The Band of the Coldstream Guards played before the match to help reinforce the sense of occasion. Most importantly, however, this was the first time ever that Town had staged a First Division match at Portman Road. The modified and enlarged North Stand had recently been completed and the ground now had an increased capacity of some 29,000. All stand seats were sold out, though in the end the attendance was less than 22,000.

Manchester City came to Portman Road on the back of a 3–1 home win over Leicester and a 4–3 success at Craven Cottage. In the close season manager Les McDowell had spent £45,000 on Kennedy from Kilmarnock and had also secured the services of Blackburn's top scorer for 1960/61 Peter Dobing. The City team was as follows: Trautmann; Betts and Leivers; Cheetham, Ewing and Kennedy; Barlow, Dobing, Baker, Hayes and Wagstaffe.

Bert Trautmann was playing his 451st game for City while Ewing was now in his thirteenth season with the club. Bill Leivers, who nine years later would manage Cambridge United into the Football League, had been in City's FA Cup winning side of 1956 as had Trautmann who famously broke his neck and played on. City's Gerry Baker would later play for Town, but unfortunately not today. Full-back Barry Betts was City captain.

The Town team was unchanged from the previous two games, reading: Bailey; Carberry and Malcolm; Elsworthy, Nelson and Baxter; Leadbetter, Moran, Crawford, Phillips and Stephenson. The referee was the wonderfully named Mr M.A. Fussey of Retford.

The *Evening Star* headline for this game read 'two late goals shattered Ipswich hopes', and the game was described as a 'freak' with 'freak decisions'. It certainly was somewhat freakish that Manchester should score all six goals. That might indicate that they deserved their win but the *Star* lamented Town's bad luck and added that they were by no means outclassed, though it was a worry that they had played as well as they knew how in three matches but had only one point to show for it.

Although Town had a decent share of the possession and dominated virtually the entire second half of this game, they were too predictable and the Manchester City team were able to counter their moves all too easily. Moran and Crawford, Town's inside forwards, did not have good games though the centre-halves Elsworthy, Nelson and Baxter were apparently solid despite conceding four goals.

The first goal came after only thirteen minutes. City troubled Town on the flanks and, after a couple of near misses, Peter Dobing weaved his way into the middle; as Town waited for him to push it out wide he unexpectedly turned inside and found Barlow through a gap and Barlow duly scored. After thirty-four minutes Leadbetter beat Trautmann but the effort was ruled out through an offside decision. But Town pressed on and were rewarded when City captain Betts attempted a back-pass that he instead lobbed over Trautmann into the net. Town's joy was short-lived, however, as Hayes, who along with Dobing displayed a great deal of quality all afternoon, took advantage of a ragged Town rearguard to put City in the lead again. Then, with half time approaching, Leadbetter cut in from the right and shot across the goal. The shot may have gone inside the far post of its own accord but that became academic as full-back Ewing stuck out a foot to divert the ball directly into the goal, leaving keeper Trautmann thumping the ground in frustration.

City had to defend desperately in the second half as Stephenson, Phillips and Baxter all came close to scoring. The game had entered its last five minutes as Elsworthy attempted to play the ball out of defence to Moran; his pass hit the referee Mr Fussey and fell to Bill Leivers. Although injured and restricted in his movement, Leivers still managed to find Dobing who promptly scored. A minute later Dobing repeated the dose to wrap up the points for City, leaving Alf Ramsey to declare that Town had lacked finishing and tackling. Town would need to improve if they were to get anything from their next game; the return match against Burnley.

The day's other First Division scores went like this:

Aston Villa	3–1	Chelsea
Burnley	3–1	Bolton Wanderers
Cardiff City	3–2	Blackpool
Fulham	2–1	Everton
Leicester City	1–0	West Bromwich Albion
Manchester United	6–1	Blackburn Rovers
Nottingham Forest	2–0	Sheffield United
Sheffield Wednesday	5–1	Birmingham City
Tottenham Hotspur	4–3	Arsenal
Wolverhampton Wanderers	3–2	West Ham United

Match No. 4
Tuesday 29 August 1961
Venue: Portman Road
Ipswich Town 6–2 Burnley   Attendance: 23,835

Ken Malcolm had strained a knee in the match against Manchester City so Alf Ramsey was forced to change the team for the first time this season. Although it had been thought that Billy Baxter might be moved to the vacant full-back position, with Reg Pickett being drafted at right-half, this would have upset the rhythm that the team had developed over the past three matches and Baxter was playing so well at half-back. So it was that Alf Ramsey brought in John Compton at full-back, although he had previously only ever played three games for Town, all at half-back. Compton had previous Division One experience, however, with Chelsea. The Town team therefore lined up as follows: Bailey; Carberry and Compton; Elsworthy, Nelson and Baxter; Leadbetter, Moran, Crawford, Phillips and Stephenson.

As for Burnley, manager Harry Potts recalled England under-23 international John Angus to the side in place of Joyce, and Towers replaced the injured Harris. After beating Ipswich at Turf Moor Burnley had gone on to beat Bolton Wanderers 3–1 and so, having drawn 2–2 at Highbury on the opening day of the season, were unbeaten in their first three games. Burnley lined up like this: Blacklaw; Angus and Elder; Adamson, Cummings and Miller; Connelly, McIlroy, Pointer, Robson and Towers. The referee was Mr K. Stokes of Newark.

What a game this proved to be; it was as if having played well for little or no reward in their previous three fixtures, Town were determined to claim a result, and how they did so. From the kick-off Town played at a furious pace, unsettling Burnley who tried to slow things down, but to no avail. Burnley were crushed and the wonder was that Town had not managed to score even more goals. The accurate, but less than snappy, headline in the *Evening Star* read, 'six-goal Ipswich rock mighty Burnley in great game'.

Town scored after only three minutes of this thrilling match when Crawford's shot beat Cummings. But the lead lasted for only seven minutes as Jimmy McIlroy flicked in Towers' cross. However, no sooner had Burnley equalised than they scored again, but in their own goal, as Miller stuck out a foot to deflect Stephenson's shot which would otherwise have gone a yard past the far post. Before half time Moran scored his first goal for the club courtesy of a pull back from Ray Crawford to make the score 3–1.

Ipswich's superiority continued after the restart with Phillips and Crawford claiming a goal each before Jimmy Leadbetter completed the Town scoring with a shot that caught an edge off a Burnley defender on its way through to the net. For what it was worth Burnley received a second consolation goal near the end when Elsworthy put the ball in his own net when trying to block Connelly's effort.

At last Town had shown that they could win in Division One and against one of the very best teams the league could offer, a side that everyone confidently expected would be a Championship contender. But Town had not simply claimed their first win in Division One; they had won comprehensively and had humiliated their visitors. Alf Ramsey's decision to play John Compton had been vindicated as Compton had fitted into the team seamlessly and Mr Ramsey was full of praise for him.

These were the other midweek results in Division One that saw August draw to a close:

28 August

Blackburn Rovers	1–1	Blackpool
Sheffield United	1–0	Cardiff City
West Ham United	2–1	Tottenham Hotspur
Wolverhampton Wanderers	2–2	Aston Villa

29 August

Arsenal	4–4	Leicester City

30 August

Birmingham City	1–1	Nottingham Forest
Bolton Wanderers	4–3	Sheffield Wednesday
Chelsea	2–0	Manchester United
Everton	3–1	West Bromwich Albion
Manchester City	2–1	Fulham

The first month of the season had come to an end with Town having the following record: played 4, won 1, drawn 1, lost 2, goals for 10, goals against 10, points 3.

In their first match away at Bolton Wanderers, Town had produced a perhaps understandably tentative start as they felt their way into the higher standard of First Division Football. In their next game at Burnley they had lost narrowly in a superb game to one of the main Championship contenders. The result of Town's first home game, versus Manchester City, had been a disappointment although City had begun the season most impressively winning all of their opening four fixtures. With just one point from three games it might have looked as if the dire predictions for Town's fortunes would prove accurate, but this obscured the fact that Town had played reasonably in their first game and very well indeed in the next. Happily their fourth fixture had then shown their true potential as in the return match against Burnley at Portman Road they had thrashed one of the finest sides in the country. Surely this was an early indication that Ipswich Town were not the relegation fodder the pundits had predicted them to be.

The complete league table at the end of the first month of the season (albeit not a full month) looked like this:

	P	W	D	L	F	A	Pts	Goal Ave.
Manchester City	4	4	0	0	13	7	8	1.86
Sheffield Wednesday	4	3	0	1	14	7	6	2.00
Nottingham Forest	4	2	2	0	7	4	6	1.75
Manchester United	4	2	1	1	10	6	5	1.67
Tottenham Hotspur	4	2	1	1	9	8	5	1.13
Sheffield United	4	2	1	1	4	4	5	1.00
Burnley	4	2	1	1	11	12	5	0.92
Everton	4	2	0	2	6	5	4	1.20
Cardiff City	4	1	2	1	4	4	4	1.00
Arsenal	4	1	2	1	10	10	4	1.00
West Ham United	4	1	2	1	7	7	4	1.00
Ipswich Town	4	1	1	2	11	10	3	1.10
Wolverhampton Wanderers	3	1	1	1	6	6	3	1.00
Aston Villa	3	1	1	1	5	5	3	1.00
Chelsea	4	1	1	2	7	8	3	0.88
Blackpool	4	1	1	2	6	7	3	0.86
Leicester City	4	1	1	2	6	8	3	0.75
Bolton Wanderers	4	1	1	2	7	10	3	0.70
Birmingham City	4	1	1	2	5	9	3	0.56
Fulham	4	1	0	3	7	9	2	0.78
West Bromwich Albion	4	1	0	3	3	6	2	0.50
Blackburn Rovers	4	0	2	2	3	9	2	0.33

Meanwhile . . .
The world carried on elsewhere, strangely oblivious to events in the First Division of the Football League. In Ipswich itself the Rogers & Hammerstein musical *South Pacific* played at the Odeon cinema in Lloyds Avenue, which also played host to Elvis Presley, or at least his celluloid image, in *Wild in the Country*. The Suffolk Greyhound derby had been run at the West Suffolk Stadium in Bury St Edmunds with the trainer of the winning dog receiving their prize from Town's Andy Nelson; the dog's name was Wagon Train. At Foxhall Stadium the England Lions Speedway team raced the Australia Kangaroos. You could catch up with the latest Big Beat and Jazz sounds at the Savoy while if you lived 'over Stoke' you might take a drink on Wherstead Road at the Uncle Tom's Cabin pub as it reopened its doors after a refurbishment in which the bar and smoke room had been knocked into one.

In the world beyond Ipswich a painting by Goya of the Duke of Wellington had been stolen from the National Gallery. A person in Norfolk was reported in the local papers as having sent a ransom note to the police, but so had several hundred other people.

The police enquiry into the infamous A6 murder continued and thirty-six people were arrested after a riot in Middlesbrough. Still further afield the United Nations sent in troops to keep the peace in the Congo and, also in Africa, Dr Hastings Banda's Malawi Congress Party won control in the Nyasaland parliament. But the dominant story was probably the increasing tension between the Western nations and the Soviet bloc over the testing of nuclear weapons that came to focus on Berlin. On 30 August the Geneva conference called to discuss the banning of nuclear weapons testing failed to reach any agreement. Perhaps to ram home the point that no agreement had been met, the very next day the Soviet Union announced their resumption of nuclear weapons tests.

Musically, the 1961/62 football season began with Helen Shapiro topping the charts, or hit parade as it was then, with 'You Don't Know'. It was only on the final day of the month that there was a new number one with John Leyton taking over in pole position with 'Johnny Remember Me'.

September

Match No. 5
Saturday 2 September 1961
Venue: The Hawthorns
West Bromwich Albion 1–3 Ipswich Town   Attendance: 19,016

West Bromwich Albion provided Town's next opponents and were another team they had never met previously. Albion were an established First Division team having been ever-present there since 1949. Since the First World War they had spent just eight out of the thirty-five seasons outside Division One. In 1961 they had finished in the mid-table obscurity of tenth position but they nevertheless had a reputation as a 'good footballing' side.

The Baggies had made a poor start to the 1961/62 season having lost at Leicester (1–0) and Everton (3–1) and at home to Sheffield Wednesday (2–0). Their only success so far had been at The Hawthorns versus Everton (2–0). Prior to the game Alf Ramsey was quoted as saying, 'I feel we shall be happy playing against them and may do well.' Mr Ramsey's words turned out to be truly prophetic as Town claimed the points and recorded their first away win in the First Division.

Town lined up as they had done in their previous game against Burnley, the team being: Bailey; Carberry and Compton; Elsworthy, Nelson and Baxter; Leadbetter, Moran, Crawford, Phillips and Stephenson.

The West Bromwich side featured a certain Bobby Robson, ostensibly in the half-back line but he actually played as an inside forward. One of the full-backs was Don Howe who would later go on to be England coach. This was the Albion team: Wallace; Howe and Williams; Robson, Jones and Drury; Jackson, Hope, Smith, Kevan and Clark. The referee was Mr G. McCabe of Sheffield.

Although Ipswich won, the match was an extremely poor one and the *Evening Star* saw it primarily as a victory by the Town defence; their headline read 'defence takes honours at The Hawthorns'. Much of the blame for the poor spectacle could be attributed to the conditions, however. It was a very hot day for watching, let alone playing football and the pitch at The Hawthorns was both hard and bumpy.

For the first twenty minutes West Bromwich Albion battered away at Ipswich without making any impression. While they had plenty of possession they had few ideas about how to do anything with the ball that might be likely to lead to a goal. They played a new formation known as the 'new deal game' which was more like the modern 4-3-3 formation.

With twenty minutes gone Town had their first real attack of any note and promptly took the lead. Billy Baxter booted a long ball up into the penalty box from the right-hand side. The Baggies' keeper Wallace simply watched the ball sail over him and though he began to scramble backwards to claim it, he lost out to Ray Crawford who headed the ball back over him for Doug Moran to prod over the goal line.

The game continued in much the same vein with Town resisting against West Brom's guileless attacking play until the forty-second minute when Crawford cut in from the right wing, nutmegging Williams the full-back. It looked odds on that Crawford would then pull the ball back but instead he ran on to wallop the ball past Wallace into the net for an excellent solo goal.

Despite continuing not to impress, West Bromwich pulled a goal back in the sixty-second minute when Jackson beat Bailey, although there was a strong suspicion that he had controlled the ball with his hand. The game rumbled on provoking a slow handclap from the home supporters. Finally Leadbetter centred and Wallace's judgement was perhaps again at fault as he stayed on his line. Ted Phillips jumped to beat Jones in the air, though neither actually got a head to the ball, and so it fell to Doug Moran who volleyed sharply through a gap to claim his second goal of the game and cement the victory for Ipswich.

For Town, Crawford was said to have played well, particularly in the second half, but Phillips and Elsworthy were not at their best. The plaudits were reserved for Carberry and more especially Compton. It was a calm, assured performance from the defence with club captain Andy Nelson being in commanding form.

With five games played, Town had moved another two places up the First Division table to ninth. These were the other Division One results on Saturday 2 September:

Birmingham City	1–5	Leicester City
Blackburn Rovers	2–1	Wolverhampton Wanderers
Blackpool	2–3	Manchester United
Bolton Wanderers	2–1	Arsenal
Chelsea	0–0	Fulham
Everton	0–4	Sheffield Wednesday
Manchester City	1–3	Burnley
Sheffield United	0–2	Aston Villa
Tottenham Hotspur	3–2	Cardiff City
West Ham United	3–2	Nottingham Forest

Match No. 6
Tuesday 5 September 1961
Venue: Portman Road
Ipswich Town 2–1 Blackburn Rovers   Attendance: 24,928

In the 1960/61 season Blackburn Rovers had finished eighth in Division One. They had spent only five of the fifteen seasons since the Second World

War in Division One and had last been promoted to the top flight just three years before in 1958. There were no Jack Walker millions back then and Blackburn Rovers were just another Lancashire mill town side waiting to mirror the decline of 'King Cotton'. During the close season Blackburn had sold Northern Ireland international Derek Dougan to Aston Villa and the previous season's top scorer Peter Dobing to Manchester City. However, they still fielded a smattering of international players including McGrath and Haverty of Eire, and England regular Bryan Douglas. They had recently signed Chris Crowe, an England under-23 man, from Leeds United, and full-back Keith Newton would later play for the full England side, although not until 1966. In addition, Ronnie Clayton had won 35 England caps between 1956 and 1960, some as captain.

For this game at Portman Road, Rovers manager Jack Marshall selected the following: Else; Bray and Newton; Clayton, Woods and McGrath; Isherwood, Crowe, Pickering, Douglas and Haverty.

The Ipswich team was the same one that had been victorious at The Hawthorns on the previous Saturday: Bailey; Carberry and Compton; Elsworthy, Nelson and Baxter; Leadbetter, Moran, Crawford, Phillips and Stephenson.

This game was hard fought and the *Evening Star* headline read 'Ipswich victorious in mighty battle by odd goal'. In the opening ten minutes or so Town looked dangerous though Blackburn succeeded in testing Roy Bailey with a couple of long-range efforts. The first goal arrived after just thirteen minutes. Roy Stephenson hoofed the ball forward which resulted in both Ted Phillips and Doug Moran getting in shots from which the ball then rebounded to the approaching Roy Stephenson who volleyed the ball in to make it 1–0 to Ipswich.

On twenty-two minutes Town succeeded in doubling their advantage. Moran and Leadbetter progressed down the left, Leadbetter then pulled the ball back, rolling it into the path of the on-rushing Ted Phillips who shot powerfully with his right foot into the net.

The scoring was completed on forty-one minutes when Billy Baxter tackled Bryan Douglas from behind and the referee, Mr K.G. Aston of Ilford, adjudged that a foul had been committed. This was not a popular decision with the crowd who roundly booed Mr Aston. As the *Evening Star* sports editor wrote, somewhat quaintly, 'Mr Aston was consigned to perdition and no half larks.' Douglas got up to convert the spot-kick with a fierce drive.

Blackburn played with a lot of skill and produced some subtle well-worked attacks but Town's defence coped well, although they did let in Crowe who managed, however, to lift the ball over the crossbar from no more than a yard out. Overall Town deserved their win on the strength of their first-half performance, but Alf Ramsey was moved to write in his programme notes for the next home game, 'We seemed to be unsettled by the penalty which brought Rovers right back into the game.' With the points won, however, the only worry after the match was an injury to Roy Bailey's thigh.

After six games Town had risen to sixth position in the league table. The other results from the midweek fixtures in Division One were as follows:

4 September
Blackpool   2–0   West Ham United
Sheffield United   1–1   Tottenham Hotspur

5 September
Burnley   2–0   Leicester City

6 September
Cardiff City   5–2   Chelsea
Everton   0–2   Manchester City
Fulham   2–2   Bolton Wanderers
West Bromwich Albion   0–0   Birmingham City

Match No. 7
Saturday 9 September 1961
Venue: Portman Road
Ipswich Town 4–1 Birmingham City   Attendance: 20,017

Birmingham City had finished nineteenth in Division One in each of the previous two seasons. This was their seventh consecutive season in the top flight and their ninth out of the sixteen since league football began again after the Second World War. Under manager Gil Merrick Birmingham were set to inhabit the lower reaches of the league table again in 1961/62 and came into this game at Portman Road on the back of a 5–1 home defeat to Leicester City.

Birmingham City lined up as follows: Withers; Foster and Allen; Watts, Smith and Beard; Hellawell, Bloomfield, Harris, Singer and Taylor.

Ipswich were unchanged for the fourth consecutive game with Roy Bailey's thigh injury from the midweek game apparently not being a problem; this therefore was Town's team: Bailey; Carberry and Compton; Elsworthy, Nelson and Baxter; Leadbetter, Moran, Crawford, Phillips and Stephenson. The referee was Mr A.L. Mason of Maidstone.

As comprehensive a victory as that over Burnley, this result prompted the *Evening Star* to run their match report under the banner 'Birmingham bewildered by vastly better side'. The writing was on the wall for Birmingham City after only two minutes as Ray Crawford collected a long through-pass from Larry Carberry and rounded Smith in the Brummies' goal to score. The game was being played at a wildly quick pace and in the early stages Birmingham were giving as good as they got, so much so that ten minutes after Town's goal they were on level terms with Singer scoring after

Bloomfield created the opening for him. Parity lasted only a further seven minutes however, until Ted Phillips lashed a twenty-five-yard shot past Withers. Thereafter, Town took control of the game.

At 2–1 up at half time, Town went further ahead in the second half when Jimmy Leadbetter robbed a sluggish Birmingham defender before setting Ted Phillips away to score his second. With the two-goal cushion Town's play became less urgent, to the annoyance of the home support, and the defence had to work hard, with Compton showing his ability once again. Billy Baxter headed out from under the crossbar while Birmingham's Bloomfield had two shots cleared off the line. However, Birmingham had a tendency to over elaborate and generally they lacked incisiveness.

With Birmingham still chasing the match gamely, but ineffectively, and Town strolling, the contest was finally killed off after Roy Stephenson forced a corner. From Stephenson's low cross, Billy Baxter drew the attention of the Birmingham defenders allowing Doug Moran to score from close in. Man of the match for Town had been Roy Stephenson whose direct play repeatedly carved out openings in the Birmingham rearguard.

The win pushed Town up to fifth place in the Division One table with nine points from seven games. The day's other results were as follows:

Arsenal	3–0	Manchester City
Aston Villa	2–4	West Ham United
Burnley	3–1	West Bromwich Albion
Cardiff City	1–2	Bolton Wanderers
Chelsea	6–1	Sheffield United
Ipswich Town	4–1	Birmingham City
Leicester City	2–0	Everton
Manchester United	1–0	Tottenham Hotspur
Nottingham Forest	1–2	Blackburn Rovers
Sheffield Wednesday	1–1	Fulham
Wolverhampton Wanderers	2–2	Blackpool

League Cup First Round
Monday 11 September 1961
Venue: Portman Road
Ipswich Town 4–2 Manchester City   Attendance: 14,919

The Town team for this, only Town's second ever League Cup tie, lined up as follows: Hall; Carberry and Compton: Baxter, Nelson and Elsworthy: Stephenson, Moran, Crawford, Phillips and Leadbetter.

The Manchester City team was: Trautmann; Betts and Sear; Cheetham, Ewing and Kennedy; Barlow, Dobing, Hannah, Hayes and Wagstaffe. The referee was Mr P. Bye.

Roy Bailey was in hospital with a thigh injury sustained in the previous Saturday's game versus Birmingham City and Wilf Hall stood in for him. Ipswich scored first after twenty-nine minutes when Doug Moran latched onto a through-pass and beat the City goalkeeper, Trautmann. Town went 2–0 up just six minutes later and it was Moran again – this time he rounded Trautmann before scoring. Ray Crawford drove in a shot from an angle just a minute before half time to put Town in full control.

City staged something of a comeback in the second half, however; firstly Barrie Betts converted a penalty after Billy Baxter fouled Joe Hayes just three minutes after the restart. Then, on fifty-four minutes, John Compton deflected a header from Roy Cheetham into the net. But the game was wrapped up for Ipswich just ten minutes later as Ray Crawford claimed his second goal of the night to be sure Town would have a place in the second round draw.

Match No. 8
Saturday 16 September 1961
Venue: Goodison Park
Everton 5–2 Ipswich Town   Attendance: 35,259

Everton were (and still are) First Division stalwarts, being founder members of the Football League in 1888 and having spent just four seasons outside the top division since then. They had, however, been in Division Two comparatively recently, having gained promotion in 1954 after three seasons 'down below'. Everton were a developing and improving side under manager Harry Catterick. After several seasons finishing in the bottom third of the table the Toffees had finished fifth in 1961 and would go on to improve on that in 1962. Eventually in 1963 Everton would be destined to take over the mantle of league champions from Town. Despite having not won a trophy since 1939, Everton were still a 'big club' and had recently spent some £250,000 on players – a huge sum. The gate of over 35,000 was the biggest that Town had so far played before in Division One and only two larger crowds would watch Town before the season's end.

While Town had never before encountered Everton in a league match, they had played at Goodison Park in the FA Cup third round back in 1953, losing 3–2 having led 2–1 at half time.

For this afternoon's game Ipswich were without the services of first-choice keeper Roy Bailey. Bailey had received a bruised thigh in the match at home to Blackburn and suffered a further knock in the Birmingham game resulting in his having to receive hospital treatment. Wilf Hall had taken Bailey's place in the League Cup match against Manchester City the previous Monday and would do so for the next four fixtures, three of which were league games. The Town team therefore read as follows: Hall; Carberry and Compton; Nelson, Elsworthy and Baxter; Stephenson, Moran, Crawford, Phillips and Leadbetter.

Everton had suffered several injuries to first-choice players in the season to this point and lined up like this: Dunlop; Parker and Thomson; Gabriel, Labone and Harris; Bingham, Young, Wignall, Temple and Fell.

Town travelled to the game on the day of the match and stayed over at Southport for the fixture at Blackburn on the following Monday. It was not to be a good day for Town and they ended well beaten. The headline in the *Evening Star* read 'Everton superior in almost every department'. The report suggested that Everton's wingers Bingham and Fell plus inside forwards Temple, who scored a hat trick, and Young had been particularly effective while the Town had been sadly disappointing in these positions. Added to this Gabriel and Harris had kept Phillips and Moran in check and Brian Labone (a future England international) had dominated Ray Crawford.

Of the Town team only Roy Stephenson and Andy Nelson emerged with much credit, but Wilf Hall made several fine saves and stood no chance with any of the goals. Alf Ramsey was to write in his programme notes for Town's next home game, 'All our players, with the notable exception of Wilf Hall, were somewhat off-colour,' in what he described as 'a very disappointing display.'

Everton took the lead in the eighteenth minute through Temple and looked the likely winners from thereon. Temple added a second on the half hour and two minutes into the second half provided the pass from which Young scored. Twenty-two minutes later Billy Bingham, future manager of Everton and Northern Ireland, grabbed Everton's fourth.

With the game seemingly over Ipswich now staged a small but pointless recovery. On seventy-two minutes some lax Everton defending, plus some skill from Moran, let in Ted Phillips. Five minutes later the arrears were reduced further as Doug Moran headed home a Roy Stephenson free-kick. But Town could not manage anything more than that and with six minutes remaining it was Everton who completed the scoring as Temple claimed his hat-trick.

The referee was Mr P.G. Brandwood of Barnsley and the defeat saw Ipswich sink two places to seventh in the Division One table. These were the other results in Division One for Saturday 16 September.

Birmingham City	2–6	Burnley
Blackburn Rovers	4–2	Aston Villa
Blackpool	1–3	Nottingham Forest
Cardiff City	1–2	Manchester United
Fulham	2–1	Leicester City
Manchester City	2–1	Bolton Wanderers
Sheffield United	1–0	Sheffield Wednesday
Tottenham Hotspur	1–0	Wolverhampton Wanderers
West Bromwich Albion	4–0	Arsenal
West Ham United	2–1	Chelsea

Match No. 9
Monday 18 September 1961
Venue: Ewood Park
Blackburn Rovers 2–2 Ipswich Town   Attendance: 19,904

The Town team was unchanged for this second away game in three days against Lancashire opposition. Town had beaten Blackburn just a fortnight before at Portman Road and the Rovers side was not greatly altered from the one they had sent out on that Tuesday evening.

Blackburn lined up like this: Reeves; Bray and Newton; Clayton, Woods and McEvoy; Isherwood, Crowe, Lawther, Douglas and Haverty.

The Town team was: Hall; Carberry and Compton; Nelson, Elsworthy and Baxter; Stephenson, Moran, Crawford, Phillips and Leadbetter. The referee was Mr R.H. Windle of Chesterfield.

This was a game that, if only they had been a bit sharper in front of goal, Town could have won. It was nevertheless a huge improvement on their performance two days earlier at Goodison Park. Town attacked from the very outset and as early as the second minute a chance was squandered. Blackburn captain Maurice Woods let in Leadbetter who dallied and tried to place the ball, allowing keeper Tom Reeves to save with his legs.

The breakthrough came after thirteen minutes when Woods was again the culprit as he handled Stephenson's corner to present Town with their first penalty of the season. In typical style Ted Phillips thundered the ball past Reeves. Town were good value for their lead with their half-back line in confident mood restricting Blackburn to long shots from Chris Crowe, Keith Newton and Bill Lowther, Wilf Hall saving well from the latter.

At the other end Baxter had a shot from distance and Elsworthy, who was enjoying space in midfield, sent a curling shot past the far post. With five minutes to go until half time, however, Town lost their grip somewhat. Having received a pass from Bryan Douglas, Lawther shot to Wilf Hall's right from eighteen yards and scored. Then, just before half time, Town had a narrow escape when Roy Isherwood shot over the bar from a good position.

A more rugged second half saw Ipswich spurning chances still, with Compton volleying over and on the hour Ray Crawford, who had had a quiet game, rattled the side-netting at the end of a fine passing move. Ted Phillips then beat Reeves with a shot only for it to be cleared off the line by Keith Newton.

After creating so many chances it was harsh that Town should fall behind on seventy-three minutes. The goal, however, was a spectacular effort with Matthew McEvoy's thirty-yard volley going in off the inside of the post. But Town only had to wait a further six minutes for their just reward. Compton chipped across the face of the goal; Reeves got to it first and punched the ball out, but only into the face of the on-rushing Ted Phillips, off whom the ball cannoned into the net. The *Evening Star* headline read 'Phillips scores fantastic equaliser at Ewood Park'.

Phillips may not have known much about that second goal but his brace at Ewood Park made him joint top scorer in Division One with nine strikes. The point Ted Phillips had rescued restored Town to sixth place in the table. The other results from the full programme of midweek fixtures turned out as follows:

18 September

Aston Villa	1–1	Manchester United
West Ham United	2–2	Blackpool

19 September

Nottingham Forest	3–1	Wolverhampton Wanderers

20 September

Birmingham City	1–2	West Bromwich Albion
Bolton Wanderers	2–3	Fulham
Chelsea	2–3	Cardiff City
Leicester City	2–6	Burnley
Manchester City	1–3	Everton
Sheffield Wednesday	1–1	Arsenal

Match No. 10
Saturday 23 September 1961
Venue: Portman Road
Ipswich Town 2–4 Fulham   Attendance: 23,050

Fulham came to Portman Road on the back of a 3–2 success over Bolton Wanderers at Burnden Park. Theirs was a team containing some rich talent in the form of a clutch of under-23 and full England internationals including goalkeeper Tony Macedo, full-backs George Cohen (a future World Cup winner) and John Langley, half-back Alan Mullery and their mercurial inside forward and captain Johnny Haynes (Haynes was of course famous for being the first footballer in England to earn £100 a week). Fulham did not have much of a First Division pedigree, however, having only won promotion two and a half years before in 1959. Previously they had spent most of the years since 1945 in Division Two, but for three seasons in the top flight between 1949 and 1952. Despite their gifted players Fulham were destined to struggle in the 1961/62 season, eventually finishing twentieth. Their tenancy in the top division would then last only another six seasons until eventual relegation in 1968.

For Ipswich, Roy Bailey had been discharged from hospital three days before the game but had not yet resumed training. Ken Malcolm was still in hospital with sciatica. The Town team lined up like this: Hall; Carberry and Compton; Baxter, Nelson and Elsworthy; Stephenson, Moran, Crawford, Phillips and Leadbetter.

Fulham were: Macedo; Cohen and Langley; Mullery, Dodgin and Low; Key, O'Connell, Cook, Haynes and Chamberlain. The referee was Mr J.E. Cooke of Waterbeach.

The headline in the *Evening Star* read 'brilliant Haynes leads Fulham to decisive victory' and the verdict was that Johnny Haynes had given a magnificent performance playing at a level slightly higher than everyone else. He was always able to create that little bit of extra time and space that made everything he did look easy and every pass smooth and effortless. Ipswich for their part simply did not mark Haynes tightly enough and only played fitfully. Roy Bailey's presence in goal was perhaps missed as Wilf Hall did not handle the ball cleanly and the defence looked hesitant and uncertain. Roy Stephenson, who had played well in recent matches, received little of the ball and despite his attempts to win possession for himself in the second half, he remained ineffective.

Despite all of this, Town actually had the better of the first half. Roy Stephenson had already hit a post with an overhead kick that had then bounced along the goal line, when on twenty-two minutes his corner was headed in by Ray Crawford to give Town the lead. This advantage lasted until shortly before half time when Cook headed in a corner from Key at the other end.

Though the first half had ended level the second belonged to Fulham and ultimately they deserved their victory. With the half only seven minutes old they took the lead when George Cohen collected a pass from O'Connell before hitting a drive past Wilf Hall. Just five minutes later Haynes extended the lead after some clever quick passing.

With twenty minutes left Town got back into the game, albeit only briefly, when keeper Tony Macedo failed to gather a shot from Roy Stephenson; the ball ran loose to Ray Crawford who despatched it into the net. Almost immediately, however, Fulham restored their two-goal cushion with a header from O'Connell. Thereafter Ted Phillips shot against a post, but otherwise Town did not come close to avoiding their second home defeat of the campaign.

The result of this match left Town without a victory against Fulham in eight attempts. Town dropped to eighth place in the table with ten points from ten games, seven points behind leaders and favourites to lift the Championship, Burnley, who were three points clear of second-placed Manchester United.

These were the other Division One results on Saturday 23 September:

Arsenal	1–1	Birmingham City
Aston Villa	5–0	Blackpool
Bolton Wanderers	3–2	West Bromwich Albion
Burnley	2–1	Everton

Chelsea	1–1	Blackburn Rovers
Leicester City	1–0	Sheffield Wednesday
Manchester United	3–2	Manchester City
Nottingham Forest	2–0	Tottenham Hotspur
Sheffield United	1–4	West Ham United
Wolverhampton Wanderers	1–1	Cardiff City

There was one midweek fixture in Division One before Town played their next match on the following Saturday.

27 September
Wolves   2–1   Nottingham Forest

Match No. 11
Saturday 30 September 1961
Venue: Hillsborough
Sheffield Wednesday 1–4 Ipswich Town   Attendance: 26,565

Town's next game renewed their acquaintance with Sheffield Wednesday, though they had in fact only been to Hillsborough once before. Since league football resumed in 1946 Wednesday had been something of a yo-yo team. After starting the post-war years in Division Two they gained promotion in 1950 only to be relegated the following season before winning the Second Division a year later in 1952. They were back in Division Two by August 1955 but won the division yet again that season. Another relegation in 1958 was followed by a third Division Two title success a year later. Back in Division One for the 1959/60 season the Owls had finished fifth and then in 1961 had been runners-up to Tottenham Hotspur. They represented fairly strong opposition therefore and were particularly acclaimed for their strong defence that included England keeper Peter Springett and centre-half Peter Swan. Swan and fellow centre-half John Kay would later be shamed in the notorious 'match-fixing' scandal when they were found guilty of having thrown the game versus Ipswich in December 1962 that Town won 2–0.

This game was Ted Phillips' 200th for Town and Andy Nelson's 100th. The teams were as follows – Sheffield Wednesday: Springett; Johnson and Megson; McAnearney, Swan, Kay; and Wilkinson; Craig, Ellis, Fantham and Dobson. Ipswich Town: Hall; Carberry and Compton; Baxter, Nelson and Elsworthy; Stephenson, Moran, Crawford, Phillips and Leadbetter. The referee was Mr E. Norman of Blackpool.

The headline in the *East Anglian Daily Times* for the report on this game read 'Sheffield Wednesday feel Phillips power' and the verdict was that Ted Phillips' shooting had been the decisive factor in a game in which Wednesday's defence had been completely crushed.

Though the scoreline did not reflect it, Wednesday had put their visitors under considerable pressure for long periods of the match. However, Town had succeeded in playing a counter-attacking game to great effect with quick breaks cutting the Wednesday defence to ribbons. Crawford, Phillips, Leadbetter and Elsworthy all carried a threat that Wednesday could not handle.

Town opened the scoring after only four minutes when Ted Phillips collected a long pass from Larry Carberry. Phillips pushed the ball beyond the challenge of Swan and another defender before nutmegging keeper Springett. The second goal came not long afterwards. Ted Phillips took a throw to Larry Carberry who then crossed to Jimmy Leadbetter. Leadbetter headed the ball back to Ray Crawford who swung his right leg at the ball and connected well, lashing the ball into the net.

Wednesday managed to halve the deficit after twenty-five minutes as Dobson, Wednesday's best forward on the day, pulled the ball back for England international Fantham to bundle the ball in – sadly the reports do not confirm whether Fantham had 'ghosted' into position.

Ten minutes later Town re-established the two-goal lead when Roy Stephenson centred from the right to Doug Moran. Moran laid the ball on for Jimmy Leadbetter who was running in at speed and steered a right-foot shot just inside the far post. Wednesday fought back against Town but to no avail and Ted Phillips put the seal on the game when he burst clear on the left, beat full-back Johnson twice before blasting the ball goalwards. Springett got a hand to the ball but could do nothing to divert its progress into the net. The *Evening Star* reporter commented that he did not think he had ever seen a ball hit so hard.

Town's return to winning ways pushed them back up to sixth in the table. September ended with the club about to embark on the second round of the League Cup and with the following league record: played 11, won 5, drawn 2, lost 4, goals for 30, goals against 25, points 12. The other games played in Division One on Saturday 30 September produced these results:

Birmingham City	2–1	Bolton Wanderers
Blackburn Rovers	1–2	Sheffield United
Blackpool	4–0	Chelsea
Cardiff City	2–2	Nottingham Forest
Everton	4–1	Arsenal
Fulham	3–5	Burnley
Manchester United	0–2	Wolverhampton Wanderers
Tottenham Hotspur	1–0	Aston Villa
West Bromwich Albion	2–2	Manchester City
West Ham United	4–1	Leicester City

So ended the second month of the 1961/62 Football League season; Ipswich were doing just fine, but down the road at Colchester the local team was doing even better, albeit in Division Four, as the Us topped the table. The full First Division table at the end of September lined up like this:

	P	W	D	L	F	A	Pts	Goal Ave.
Burnley	10	8	1	1	33	19	17	1.74
Manchester United	9	6	2	1	20	12	14	1.67
West Ham United	10	5	3	2	22	17	13	1.29
Nottingham Forest	10	5	2	3	19	13	12	1.46
Manchester City	10	6	0	4	21	20	12	1.05
Fulham	10	4	3	3	19	17	11	1.12
Sheffield Wednesday	9	4	2	3	20	11	10	1.82
Ipswich Town	10	4	2	4	26	24	10	1.08
Tottenham Hotspur	9	4	2	3	14	14	10	1.00
Bolton Wanderers	10	4	2	4	19	21	10	0.90
Blackburn Rovers	10	3	4	3	15	17	10	0.88
Cardiff City	10	3	3	4	17	16	9	1.06
Leicester City	10	4	1	5	17	19	9	0.89
Aston Villa	8	3	2	3	17	14	8	1.21
Arsenal	9	2	4	3	16	18	8	0.89
Everton	10	4	0	6	15	18	8	0.83
Sheffield United	9	3	2	4	7	17	8	0.41
Chelsea	10	2	3	5	19	20	7	0.95
West Bromwich Albion	10	3	1	6	13	16	7	0.81
Wolverhampton Wanderers	9	2	3	4	13	16	7	0.81
Blackpool	10	2	3	5	15	22	7	0.68
Birmingham City	10	1	3	6	11	27	5	0.41

Meanwhile . . .

Beyond the world of football tension was continuing to mount between the USSR and the West due to the Soviets' insistence on testing nuclear weapons. On 5 September the USA didn't really help matters by announcing they were to resume underground nuclear testing. On 9 September the USSR rejected Britain and America's proposals to ban nuclear tests and just to make the point they set off a device two days later somewhere up in the Arctic Circle. As the super powers seemingly looked forward to the prospect of assured mutual destruction, on 5 September an international conference opened in Arusha, Tanganyika, on wildlife preservation showing that some people were continuing to be positive.

On 8 September French president Charles de Gaulle escaped assassination by someone who did not approve of his government's policy towards the French colony of Algeria and therefore lobbed a petrol bomb in his direction. Algeria became independent in 1962, but some things have not changed and on 29 September the Israeli army killed what were described as 'marauders' on the Gaza strip. On 18 September the United Nations secretary Dag Hammarskjold was killed in a plane crash in the Congo as he flew to arrange a ceasefire between UN and Katanga forces.

Back in Britain the Trades Union Congress was held in Portsmouth where they voted to support Britain's entry into what was then called the Common Market. They also expelled the Communist-dominated Electrical Trades Union from the TUC. Another unhappy trade union was the National Union of Teachers whose members held a one-day strike on 20 September in support of a pay claim. Also during the month the Postmaster General announced that for the first time there would be no postal delivery on Christmas Day.

Closer to home still, just a bus ride away perhaps, an Ipswich Corporation bus conductor was fined for selling 'second-hand' bus tickets to passengers and pocketing their fares. Also on the buses the council were considering putting up the fares to pay for the cost of replacing the last eighteen trolleybuses in the fleet. Each new motorbus cost £5,500.

Other local news stories included the start of the movement of some 10,000 people out of London to the 'overspill' towns of Haverhill and Thetford. An explosion in Burrell Road, Ipswich, killed the driver of a lorry transporting oxygen cylinders and at the Blackburn Rovers game at Portman Road on 6 September three Northstanders were the victims of pick-pockets who nabbed their wallets. The *Evening Star* published a football-related letter from a reader who complained that Ken Malcolm the Town full-back was in hospital with sciatica when there were other people needing treatment who had to wait because of a shortage of hospital beds – something else that hasn't changed.

Finally, if you weren't in hospital and you still had your wallet you could go shopping in the now 'completely modernised' Marks & Spencer store in Westgate Street. Alternatively you could have taken advantage of 'corset fitting week' in the 'Corset Salon' at Footmans department store (now Debenhams). If you had a bit more cash and did not need a corset, Egertons garage was advertising a black 1959 Hillman Minx De Luxe, with a heater, for £535. Unfortunately the Minx did not have a radio, but had it done so you could have listened to John Leyton giving his chart-topping rendition of 'Johnny Remember Me' which was number one in the hit parade for the whole of September but for one week when Shirley Bassey took over temporarily with 'Reach for the Stars' and 'Climb Every Mountain' – what inspiring titles these proved to be for the Town.

Finally, far away in Colombia on 2 September, a football story began with the birth of Carlos Valderrama who was destined to become one of the world's most famous footballers, largely on account of his amazing hairstyle.

October

The first Saturday in October 1961 was Saturday the seventh, but Aston Villa were alone in hosting a midweek league fixture before then and this was the result:

2 October
Aston Villa   1–0   Wolverhampton Wanderers

The following night, however, League Cup fixtures were scheduled and Ipswich, having beaten Manchester City at Portman Road in the first round, had been drawn away at Swansea Town.

League Cup Second Round
Tuesday 3 October 1961
Venue: Vetch Field
Swansea Town 3–3 Ipswich Town   Attendance: 13,541

The Swansea Town team comprised: Dwyer; Sanders and Griffiths, Johnson, Nurse and Davies P.; Jones, Davies R., Dodson, Williams H. and Williams G. Ipswich Town lined up like this: Hall; Millward and Compton; Baxter, Nelson and Elsworthy; Stephenson, Moran, Crawford, Phillips and Leadbetter. The referee was Mr R. Leafe.

Ipswich had a torrid time in the first half of this match as they contrived to give the Swans a three-goal lead in the opening twenty-five minutes. First, after just two minutes, John Compton passed the ball beyond Wilf Hall into the net. After ten minutes Andy Nelson followed Compton's example and headed Swansea further into the lead. Finally, after twenty-four minutes Swansea scored for themselves, but only just as it was the wind took a Davies cross into the net.

Fortunately for Town they did much better in the second half with Ted Phillips setting them on their way with a goal only eight minutes after the restart. Twelve minutes later Roy Stephenson cut the deficit to a single goal with the best goal of the night. There were only three minutes to go, however, when Ray Crawford took the tie to a replay as he connected with a cross from Doug Moran.

Match No. 12
Saturday 7 October 1961
Venue: Portman Road
Ipswich Town 4–2 West Ham United   Attendance: 28,059

Portman Road recorded a new highest ever attendance figure for a league match with the visit of the Hammers. This record crowd number was due to be broken three more times, however, before the season ended.

Prior to this match West Ham United were lying in second place in the First Division table behind Burnley, whose only defeat so far had been at Ipswich. This was the Hammers' fourth season in Division One, having been promoted as Second Division Champions as recently as 1958, though they were set to stay there for twenty seasons. Prior to 1958 West Ham had not been in the top division since 1932.

In 1962 West Ham United had a side graced with names that would soon become famous, though at the time they would not have realised it. Most notably the half-backs were Geoff Hurst and Bobby Moore. Famous for another reason, or perhaps infamous, would be full-back John Bond and centre-back Ken Brown, both of whom went on to manage Norwich City. Centre forward Alan Sealey was the cousin of Les Sealey who would later become a Hammers goalkeeper. West Ham United were an emerging side on the threshold of success, as they would win the FA Cup in 1964. Interestingly, manager Ron Greenwood had tried to sign Ted Phillips for the Hammers for the 1961/62 season but thankfully Alf Ramsey was having none of it.

For Ipswich Roy Bailey returned from injury, ousting Wilf Hall, but otherwise the team remained unchanged from the one that had been victorious at Hillsborough the previous Saturday. Ken Malcolm had been discharged from hospital on the previous Tuesday but John Compton's place in the team was secure. The referee was Mr P.G. Brandwood of Wolverhampton.

Ipswich Town: Bailey; Carberry and Compton; Baxter, Nelson and Elsworthy; Stephenson, Moran, Crawford, Phillips and Leadbetter.

West Ham United: Leslie; Kirkup and Bond; Hurst, Brown and Moore; Scott, Woosnam, Sealey, Dick and Musgrove.

This game was certainly not one of the more memorable fixtures of the season, except that is for the fact that Ted Phillips created a new scoring record for the Town with his 146th goal in just 202 games. The game had lasted for almost an hour before the first goal, but then there were six goals in the final third of the game. The only notable action from the first half had been two fine saves by Leslie from Ray Crawford; one effort being a diving header and the other a powerful low drive.

But then, in the fifty-seventh minute, Jimmy Leadbetter dispossessed a somewhat casual Ken Brown; Crawford received the ball and went on to score with a precise shot. Seven minutes later Town doubled their lead as Phillips' shot went under the diving Leslie and two minutes later Town were three up as Crawford collected the fallout from Phillips' twenty-five-yard shot which Leslie had been unable to hold.

West Ham pulled a goal back on seventy minutes when Sealey shot from the left, but Ted Phillips re-established Town's three-goal lead with a header. The final consolation was provided for West Ham by Musgrove who scored in the final few minutes to make the score 4–2.

The *East Anglian Daily Times* attributed the win to the fighting qualities of the Town side but especially to the double threat posed by Phillips and Crawford whom it described as 'the two most deadly marksmen in the modern English game.'

Despite the fact that six goals were scored, for most of the game the defences of both teams had held the upper hand. West Ham had seemed not to have approached the game with an attacking policy in mind and Town had been wary of West Ham's highly rated Welsh international forward Phil Woosnam. But in the end neither defence had held out, and Crawford and Phillips had proved too good for West Ham.

These were the other First Division results in full for Saturday 7 October 1961:

7 October

Arsenal	3–0	Blackpool
Birmingham City	3–6	Wolves
Everton	6–0	Nottingham Forest
Fulham	3–1	Aston Villa
Leicester City	4–1	Sheffield United
Manchester City	1–2	Cardiff City
Sheffield Wednesday	5–3	Chelsea
West Bromwich Albion	1–1	Manchester United

Friendly (inauguration of Kettering Town's new floodlights)
9 October 1961
Venue: Rockingham Road
Kettering Town 2–2 Ipswich Town   Attendance: 5,500

This match was played to officially 'open' Kettering Town's floodlights, on which they had spent £12,000. Sir Stanley Rous was the eminent guest who switched on the lights.

These were the teams – Kettering Town: Smethurst; Marston and Lawson; Parsons, Froggatt and Armour; Shaw, Ritchie, Morrow, Curran and Golding. Ipswich Town: Bailey; Carberry and Compton; Thrower, Laurel and Nelson; Stephenson, Moran, Crawford, Phillips and Leadbetter. The referee was Ken Aston of Ilford.

There were rare appearances in the Ipswich line-up for John Laurel, who only ever played six competitive first team games and Dennis Thrower, an Ipswich-born wing-half whose last competitive first team game had been in March 1957.

Kettering took a two-goal lead through Ritchie (on two minutes) and Morrow (fifty-seven minutes) but Ipswich restored their pride with two late goals inside two minutes from Ray Crawford.

Match No. 13
Saturday 14 October 1961
Venue: Bramall Lane
Sheffield United 2–1 Ipswich Town   Attendance: 22,194

Ipswich Town's next match was against the side that had finished as runners-up to them in the previous season's Second Division Championship race – Sheffield United. This was the Blades' third stint in the First Division since the Second World War, but both their previous stays had lasted only three seasons. This season United were destined to finish a creditable fifth and would last another six seasons in Division One until eventual relegation in 1968. The previous season Town had wrested the Division Two Championship from Sheffield United by a single point and crucially had won well at Bramall Lane by three goals to one. Town had fared well on Yorkshire soil in the past year and hopes were high that this would continue.

For Town, Roy Stephenson had been a slight doubt during the week owing to a thigh strain, but he was passed fit to play. Billy Baxter, who was doing his National Service in the Army, had played for his regiment in the Army Cup during the week but had come through unscathed and was ready to play.

Sheffield United made two changes to the team that had beaten Second Division Newcastle United 2–0 in a League Cup tie during the week, with Gerry Summers and Billy Russell replacing Harry Orr and Tony Wagstaffe. The teams lined up like this – Sheffield United: Hodgkinson; Coldwell and Shaw G.; Richardson, Shaw J. and Summers; Allchurch, Russell, Pace, Simpson and Hartle. Ipswich Town: Bailey; Carberry and Compton; Baxter, Nelson and Elsworthy; Stephenson, Moran, Crawford, Phillips and Leadbetter. The referee was Mr L.J. Hamer of Bolton.

This was a match from which Town should have taken both points; that they did not was due to their inability to convert the chances they created into goals. The *East Anglian Daily Times* headline read 'Ipswich Town blot their copy book' and the sports editor wrote that Town had lost to a side who were their inferior in almost every position.

Town fell behind after only twelve minutes to a goal from Russell. Derek Pace had headed Barry Hartle's centre towards the far post; Town's defenders failed to attack the ball and it fell to Russell who scored. Ipswich had their moments and played well in spells throughout the game. Indeed, they equalised after half an hour through Jimmy Leadbetter who scored with a precise shot having latched on to the rebound from an effort by Ray Crawford. At that stage of the game it seemed likely that Town would go on to take control and claim both points, despite not being at their very best. It didn't work out like that, however, as on forty-two minutes United won a free-kick just outside the penalty box after a foul by Elsworthy. Russell struck the free-kick and although Roy Bailey got both hands to it as he dived towards the far post, he could not gather the ball and Pace managed to force it over the line.

After that Town pressed for a second equaliser but it would not come. Ted Phillips blasted one chance into the side netting from ten yards after a quick move by Crawford and Leadbetter. Crawford and Moran were also guilty of misses. The last chance came three minutes from time when, during a goalmouth mêlée, a tumbling Ray Crawford managed to hook the ball against a post; it then proceeded to run along the goal line with no Town player being able to provide the final touch before Brian Richardson hacked it clear.

So it was that Town recorded their fifth defeat of the season as their thirteenth match arguably proved to be unlucky. They now lay sixth in the First Division. The top six looked like this:

	P	W	D	L	F	A	Pts
Burnley	12	9	1	2	39	34	19
West Ham United	13	7	3	3	30	23	17
Tottenham Hotspur	12	7	2	3	19	15	16
Manchester United	12	6	3	3	21	17	15
Everton	13	7	0	6	28	19	14
Ipswich Town	13	6	2	3	35	29	14

Bolton Wanderers and Tottenham Hotspur had met on the previous Monday, the only midweek fixture that week. The result of that game and the other Saturday fixtures went as follows:

9 October
Bolton Wanderers	1–2	Tottenham Hotspur

14 October
Blackburn Rovers	0–0	Arsenal
Blackpool	2–1	Bolton Wanderers
Chelsea	1–3	Leicester City
Manchester United	0–2	Birmingham City
Nottingham Forest	1–1	Fulham
Tottenham Hotspur	2–0	Man City
West Ham United	2–1	Burnley
Wolverhampton Wanderers	0–3	Everton

Four of the top six teams won, with second-placed West Ham beating top-of-the-table Burnley in the battle of the claret and blues at Upton Park. The other losers were Manchester United, who were vanquished at home by Birmingham City to the tune of two goals to nil.

Match No.14
Saturday 21 October 1961
Venue: Portman Road
Ipswich Town 3–2 Tottenham Hotspur   Attendance: 28,778

There was another record attendance at Portman Road, beating the league record set just a fortnight before, for this match against the reigning champions and FA Cup holders. This was the biggest ever attendance at Portman Road in any competition, but it was to be exceeded again before the season ended.

During the week preceding the game Jimmy Leadbetter had been suffering with a 'chill', and John Compton did not train due to a back complaint. But come Saturday both were passed fit and similarly Ted Phillips had recovered from a leg injury. Billy Baxter had played for the Army against a Football Association XI at Sunderland during the week but had not picked up any injury so Town fielded an unchanged side. It was trainer Jimmy Forsyth's 500th consecutive match as trainer since joining Town eleven years earlier.

For their part, Tottenham Hotspur were the current champions and FA Cup holders, being the first team to lift the double since Aston Villa in 1897. The Spurs side, under the management of Bill Nicholson, fielded six regular international players, most notably perhaps Danny Blanchflower (Northern Ireland), and Dave Mackay (Scotland) who would go on to manage Derby County to a league championship success in 1975. Spurs had signed their number five, Maurice Norman, from Norwich City. The two sides lined up like this – Ipswich Town: Bailey; Carberry and Compton; Baxter, Nelson and Elsworthy; Stephenson, Moran, Crawford, Phillips and Leadbetter. Tottenham Hotspur: Brown, Baker and Henry; Blanchflower, Norman and Mackay; Jones, White, Smith, Allen and Dyson. The referee was Mr Ray Tinkler of Boston.

In common with all Town's games against the top sides in their Championship-winning season, this was another classic. The sports editor in the *East Anglian Daily Times* wrote of the record Portman Road crowd being 'left wondering what is the limit to this wonderful side.' It was the force of Crawford and Phillips that tipped this game in the favour of Town, though Roy Bailey played his part with a crucial points-clinching save. This was one of those games of 'two halves' but only in as much as the first half was good and the second half better still.

It was Spurs who took the lead when after twenty-one minutes John White's swinging cross eluded Smith, only for Cliff Jones to hurl himself at the ball and send a flying header past Bailey. It took a quarter of an hour for Town to equalise. Leadbetter fed Crawford a short square pass and he in turn edged the ball forward to Phillips who lashed a shot into the net from his left boot.

On the verge of half time, however, Tottenham regained the lead with another diving header from Jones. Buoyed by their lead, the Londoners had Town on the ropes in the opening minutes of the second half in which time they played some superb football. Bailey, Baxter and Compton all saved Town in a series of frantic scrambles but on fifty-four minutes Town were level as Crawford elegantly swept home the rebound from the blocked efforts of Stephenson and Phillips. Then, within two minutes, Ray Crawford repeated the dose after he had received the ball from Roy Stephenson.

As the game entered its last ten minutes Tottenham laid siege to the Ipswich goal. Their half-backs Dave Mackay and Danny Blanchflower threw caution to the wind and went marauding upfield. Spurs displayed great skill and ability, but Town were still a constant threat to them with their more direct approach. In contrast to Blanchflower and Mackay meanwhile, Town's pairing of Elsworthy and Baxter stayed back and took few risks.

Roy Bailey took his share of credit for the result with a blinding save from White. Already on the ground, having stopped an effort from Les Allen, Bailey swung himself back to his left to gather White's shot to his chest. The momentum of the shot spun Bailey around but he held onto the ball.

After the game Bill Nicholson was quoted as saying, 'If we had had Ipswich's two goalscoring forwards we should have paralysed 'em!' Typically, Alf Ramsey used more sedate language and was reported as having said, 'It was truly a great match and a tremendous second half. Although we won and are naturally more than pleased, tribute must be paid to Tottenham – a very fine side indeed.'

Ramsey must have indeed been pleased with this victory over the club he had played for and won successive Second and First Division Championships with in 1950 and 1951 – a club who only months beforehand had become the first in the twentieth century to win the double, and who were clear favourites to at least win the league again this season.

The result took Town above Spurs into fourth place with 16 points. Above Town, though, were Everton, also with 16 points, West Ham United with 17 points and clear at the top with 21 points were Burnley. Aston Villa and Cardiff City had both played midweek home games, producing these results:

16 October

Aston Villa	1–0	Sheffield Wednesday

18 October

Cardiff City	2–2	West Bromwich Albion

21 October

Arsenal	5–1	Manchester United
Birmingham City	3–2	Chelsea
Bolton Wanderers	1–0	Wolverhampton Wanderers
Burnley	2–1	Cardiff City
Everton	1–0	Sheffield United
Fulham	2–0	West Ham United
Leicester City	0–2	Blackpool
Manchester City	3–0	Nottingham Forest
Sheffield Wednesday	1–0	Blackburn Rovers
West Bromwich Albion	1–1	Aston Villa

League Cup Second Round Replay
Tuesday 24 October 1961
Venue: Portman Road
Ipswich Town 3–2 Swansea Town   Attendance: 11,010

This was Swansea Town's fourth match in ten days and one of those matches had been in East Germany against Motor Jena in the European Cup Winners' Cup; they had lost 5–1. Swansea had qualified as the Welsh Cup holders. Perhaps because of the travelling and playing so many games in such a short period, their team at Portman Road differed quite a lot from the one they had fielded in Swansea.

The teams for this League Cup replay lined up like this – Ipswich Town: Bailey; Carberry and Compton; Baxter, Nelson and Elsworthy; Stephenson, Moran, Crawford, Phillips and Leadbetter. Swansea Town: Dwyer; Saunders and Griffiths; Johnson, Nurse and Hughes; Jones, Morgans, Dodson, Reynolds and Webster. The referee was once again Mr Leafe of Nottingham.

Despite the team changes Swansea again took an early lead and were 2–0 up after twenty-six minutes with Hughes and Reynolds the scorers. But by half time Ipswich were level. First, on thirty-eight minutes Doug Moran was brought down unnecessarily in the penalty area. As usual Ted Phillips scored; then, with a minute to go before half time, Ipswich won a free-kick from about twenty-three yards out. Swansea did not bother with a wall, perhaps fearing it would be useless against the power of Ted Phillips' shooting. Phillips did shoot, and although Dwyer went down to save well, he could only parry the ball as far as Doug Moran who swept it into the net for the equaliser.

Town had to wait until the eightieth minute for the winner when Roy Stephenson went on a run down the wing. He cut inside Nurse and receiving no further challenges he carried on towards goal and shot past Dwyer to score. Town had won, but the *East Anglian* headline said it all: 'Town scrape through'.

Match No. 15
Saturday 28 October 1961
Venue: Bloomfield Road
Blackpool 1–1 Ipswich Town   Attendance: 19,773

After beating the current league champions, the following week brought a more mundane fixture with a trip to Blackpool, who had escaped relegation by a single point the previous season. In spite of this, Blackpool had one of the strongest First Division pedigrees having not been in the Second Division since 1937. Throughout the 1950s Blackpool had finished in the top nine of the division and had been runners-up only five years earlier in 1956. Among their ranks Blackpool boasted England full-back Jimmy Armfield, now a football commentator on BBC radio. In goal Tony Waiters would later gain five England caps and centre forward Ray Charnley would also win an England call-up. Winger Steve Hill was already an England under-23 international. This season was to turn out to be one of relative mediocrity with Blackpool destined to finish thirteenth come the end of the campaign. As they went into this game the Seasiders were lying fifteenth in the table and had won their previous match 2–0 away at Leicester.

The teams lined up as follows – Blackpool: Waiters; Armfield and Martin; Crawford B., Gratrix and Durie; Hill, Peterson, Charnley, Parry and Horne. Ipswich Town: Bailey; Carberry and Compton; Baxter, Nelson and Elsworthy; Stephenson, Moran, Crawford, Phillips and Leadbetter. The referee was Mr A.W. Luty of Leeds.

After the glory of the Tottenham game this match was to prove a disappointment and the headline in the *East Anglian Daily Times* read 'half-hearted performance at Blackpool'. As had been the case in the last away match at Sheffield United, Town were the better side but were unable to claim the result their superiority suggested they deserved. To be fair to Blackpool, they were hampered by an injury to Jimmy Armfield after only twenty-three minutes. Armfield had only recently returned from injury and having gone off for treatment he returned with his leg heavily strapped. He proceeded to play as centre forward as of course there were no substitutes permitted at that time.

Not long afterwards Town took the lead, as on thirty-two minutes Phillips pushed the ball out to the right from where it was swiftly moved to the other flank. Winger Jimmy Leadbetter then sent the ball into the middle where Phillips headed it past Waiters to end the move that he had begun. The game then almost seemed to become too easy for Town but they did not press home their advantage and in fact eased up. Only Nelson, Compton and Carberry really seemed to keep going at full tempo. The forwards and half-backs all seemed somewhat lacking in enthusiasm for the game which must have been a big disappointment to the ten coach-loads of supporters who had made the long trip north to the seaside. Inevitably perhaps, Town paid the penalty for their apparent complacency and with just eight minutes to play, Blackpool's South African inside left Ray Parry equalised. Eric Peterson had lobbed the ball into Town's penalty area, and Charnley headed the ball down to Parry whose swinging boot connected with the ball to send it into the net. It only remained for Alf Ramsey to give the team a stern talking to for having let slip a point that had been there for the taking.

If there was any consolation it was that Burnley had lost (4–2 at Tottenham) so Town in fact had gained a point on the leaders, but that also meant that Tottenham had gone back ahead of Town in the league table, although at that stage still no one was thinking in terms of challenging for the Championship. The leading scorers in Division One at this stage of the season were Ted Phillips with 17 goals and Ray Crawford with 15 goals.

The day's other results were:

28 October

Aston Villa	1–3	Birmingham City
Blackburn Rovers	2–1	Leicester City
Cardiff City	1–1	Arsenal
Chelsea	1–1	Everton
Manchester United	0–3	Bolton Wanderers
Nottingham Forest	4–4	West Bromwich Albion
Sheffield United	2–2	Fulham
Tottenham Hotspur	4–2	Burnley
West Ham United	2–3	Sheffield Wednesday
Wolverhampton Wanderers	4–1	Manchester City

The full league table at the end of October panned out like this:

	P	W	D	L	F	A	Pts	Goal Ave.
Burnley	14	10	1	3	43	29	21	1.48
Tottenham Hotspur	14	8	2	4	25	20	18	1.25
Everton	15	8	1	6	30	20	17	1.50
Ipswich Town	15	7	3	5	39	32	17	1.22
Fulham	15	6	5	4	30	26	17	1.15
West Ham United	15	7	3	5	32	28	17	1.14
Sheffield Wednesday	14	7	2	5	30	21	16	1.43
Manchester City	15	7	1	7	28	30	15	0.93
Nottingham Forest	15	5	5	5	26	29	15	0.90
Manchester United	14	6	3	5	22	25	15	0.88
Arsenal	14	4	6	4	26	24	14	1.08
Cardiff City	15	4	6	5	25	24	14	1.04
Bolton Wanderers	15	6	2	7	26	27	14	0.96
Blackpool	15	5	4	6	24	27	14	0.89
Aston Villa	14	5	3	6	22	22	13	1.00
Wolverhampton Wanderers	15	5	3	7	25	25	13	1.00
Leicester City	15	6	1	8	26	29	13	0.90
Blackburn	14	4	5	5	18	21	13	0.86
Birmingham City	15	5	3	7	24	37	13	0.65
Sheffield United	14	5	3	6	14	26	13	0.54
West Bromwich Albion	15	3	6	6	23	26	12	0.88
Chelsea	15	2	4	9	26	36	8	0.72

Meanwhile . . .

There was good news in Colchester where the Us were top of the Division Four table. In Ipswich, however, there was bad news as another pub closed. The Bull Inn in Key Street was the sixteenth Ipswich pub to close in just six years; theme pubs and binge-drinking had not yet been invented in 1961.

In politics a future Prime Minister was working her way up the greasy pole as on 10 October Margaret Thatcher was appointed Joint Parliamentary Secretary at the Ministry of Pensions & Insurance. The same day negotiations also began for Britain's entry into the Common Market. Not such a good day for Chico Marx, however, who died aged seventy.

October saw the start of the Earl's Court Motor Show and on 11 October the British Motor Corporation (BMC, the forerunner of British Leyland) introduced two new models, the Wolseley Hornet and Riley Elf. These cars were really modified Minis, but rather than spoilers, fat tyres and fog lamps these cars had altogether more classy additions such as walnut fascias, chrome grilles and tail fins. Prices for these most desirable vehicles began at £672 and £693 respectively.

During the month there was talk of building a Channel tunnel, but elsewhere in Europe Soviet and United States tanks faced each other across the sector border in Berlin as tension between East and West rumbled on. Further east still, in Moscow, the body of Stalin was to be exhumed from the tomb in Red Square as his popularity came to be reassessed now that he was no longer able to purge anyone.

Three records hit the number one spot in the hit parade during the course of October. The Shadows knocked John Leyton off the top on 5 October with 'Kon-tiki' but they were ousted a week later by Michael and 'Highwayman' who in turn lasted only a week before Helen Shapiro stepped up with 'Walkin' back to happiness'.

Back in Ipswich, at the Odeon cinema you could watch the X-certificate *A Taste of Honey* starring Rita Tushingham and Dora Bryan. Today this film is probably tamer than an average episode of *Eastenders*, but its subject matter of a pregnant teenage schoolgirl, and her life with a homosexual friend and alcoholic mother meant it was not deemed fit for under-eighteens. Perhaps as an antidote against all that sin and depravity the film on view at the Gaumont was Cecil B. DeMille's epic *The Ten Commandments*.

Also in Ipswich, a piece of land was advertised for redevelopment, to be let on a ninety-nine-year lease. This three-acre site would become the infamous Greyfriars development.

Finally, a football-related story as Archie MaCauley, the Norwich manager since April 1957 resigned, and was reported as saying, 'I do not feel completely happy.' On 20 October he joined West Bromwich Albion.

November

There were no midweek First Division games prior to Ipswich's first November Saturday fixture, but one of the team, Ray Crawford, nevertheless got a game on Tuesday 1 November. Ray had been selected to represent the Football League in an inter-league game against the Irish League at Windsor Park in Belfast. A crowd of some 15,000 saw the Football League XI win 6–1 and Ray bag two goals.

Match No. 16
Saturday 4 November 1961
Venue: Portman Road
Ipswich Town 1–0 Nottingham Forest   Attendance: 19,068

The lacklustre performance at Blackpool was unfortunately to be repeated in the next match, at home to Nottingham Forest, which was not far from ending in another draw. Forest were to have an unspectacular season and would eventually escape relegation by just two places and four points. Forest had been promoted to Division One in 1957 as Division Two runners-up, but previously had not been in the top flight since 1926. So far their run in Division One had been very ordinary with their best finish being tenth in 1958. They had enjoyed a fairly recent success in the FA Cup, however, beating Luton Town in the 1959 final by two goals to one.

Facing Town today was an England international in Jeff Whitefoot, but goalkeeper Peter Grummitt and full-back Brian Grant were inexperienced and were still teenagers. Colin Booth was an England B international and Forest's record signing, from Wolverhampton Wanderers. Unusually, the Forest side included two Channel Islanders, in Richard Le Flem and Geoff Vowden. Their manager was Andy Beattie.

Ipswich Town's side that day were: Bailey; Carberry and Compton; Baxter, Nelson and Elsworthy; Stephenson, Moran, Crawford, Phillips and Leadbetter. Nottingham Forest lined up with: Grummitt; Gray and Grant; Palmer, McKinlay and Whitefoot; Vowden, Booth, Addison, Quigley and Le Flem. The referee was Mr G.W. Pullin of Bristol.

The arrival of November heralded the first blast of wintry weather and it was a cold day. Perhaps this affected the teams, but the match was reported as having been very ordinary with neither side showing any inspiration. The *East Anglian Daily Times* went so far as to say in their headline 'off form Ipswich lucky to get both points'.

The only goal of the game fell to Ipswich in the twenty-third minute. Ray Crawford headed the ball out to Jimmy Leadbetter who was in a customary wide position. Leadbetter took his time before sending a lobbed ball across the face of the goal. Ray Crawford had run on since his lay-off to Leadbetter and he jumped for the ball with a Forest player, but neither got a touch on it and it fell to Ted Phillips who scored easily.

In the second half Doug Moran came close to doubling Town's lead but his header was in turn headed off the goal line. Ted Phillips went close to scoring from a long-range shot and Booth did likewise for Forest.

Town had a fortunate escape with just twelve minutes to go when Vowden was brought down in the penalty area. Referee Pullin awarded the spot-kick but Calvin Palmer's effort was hit with little power or accuracy and Bailey was able to dive to his left and palm the shot away.

Nottingham also had two goals disallowed for offside, one of which was blatant and one less so. Grummitt made two or three decent saves in the course of the match but Town's best performers were Nelson, Compton and Carberry who were all staunch at the back. Elsewhere on the field Town seemed devoid of any sort of a game plan and lacked the organisation that had been so typical of them in previous successes.

Despite the less than thrilling performance Town were now third in the table, level on points with Everton and West Ham United, but still four behind leaders Burnley. The result left Nottingham Forest in thirteenth place.

The day's other results were as follows:

Arsenal	0–3	Chelsea
Birmingham City	1–1	Blackpool
Bolton Wanderers	2–0	Sheffield United
Burnley	3–0	Aston Villa
Everton	3–0	Tottenham Hotspur
Fulham	0–1	Cardiff City
Leicester City	3–0	Wolverhampton Wanderers
Manchester City	3–5	West Ham United
Sheffield Wednesday	3–1	Manchester United
West Bromwich Albion	4–0	Blackburn Rovers

Friendly in aid of the Haig Fund
Monday 6 November 1961
Venue: Milton Road
Cambridge City 2–5 Ipswich Town   Attendance: 5,500

Billy Baxter sat out this game and Dennis Thrower took his place, but otherwise the team was the first-choice eleven. The result looked like a handsome victory but in fact the score flattered Ipswich somewhat. The Ipswich goalscorers were Crawford (24, 80), Moran (52, 66) and Phillips (85).

Match No. 17
Saturday 11 November 1961
Venue: Molineux
Wolverhampton Wanderers 2–0 Ipswich Town   Attendance: 21,711

Town fielded an unchanged team for the sixth consecutive game as they
travelled to the Black Country and their first ever visit to Molineux. Town
had played Wolves just once before, in a friendly at Portman Road back
in 1938, and the game had ended in a 2–2 draw, but this was to be their
first competitive meeting. This was Wolverhampton Wanderers' twenty-third
consecutive season in Division One since winning Division Two in 1932.
They were still managed by Stan Cullis who had famously led them to three
Championship successes in the previous decade, most recently retaining
the title just two and a half years before in 1959. Since then Wolves had
finished second and then third. Currently, however, the Molineux side were
not reproducing that type of form and were languishing in the bottom half of
the table.

The teams lined up as follows – Wolverhampton Wanderers: Finlayson;
Stuart and Harris; Clamp, Slater and Flowers; Wharton, Mason, Murray,
Broadbent and Hinton. Ipswich Town: Bailey; Carberry and Compton;
Baxter, Nelson and Elsworthy; Stephenson, Moran, Crawford, Phillips and
Leadbetter. The referee was Mr P. Bye of Bedford.

This was not to be Town's day and this fact became all too apparent after
only six minutes when they lost Roy Stephenson with a thigh strain. The
replacement of injured players with a substitute would not be introduced
until 1965 so Town had to play out the remaining eighty-four minutes
of the match a man down. In spite of this handicap, however, they held
Wolves at bay until the last twenty minutes of the second half. In fact,
in the first half Town played very well and might have taken the lead.
Ray Crawford missed a chance with an early header and just before half
time they had a penalty appeal turned down when Harris appeared to
foul Ray Crawford. Ted Phillips worked hard but his shooting was mostly
inaccurate.

As the game wore on Town, predictably, began to tire and Wolverhampton
increasingly kept possession of the ball, which wore Ipswich down still
further. The defence played well throughout with Carberry, Compton and
Baxter all earning credit and Andy Nelson also kept a tight rein on Wolves'
centre forward Murray. On sixty-nine minutes, however, Wolves' teenage
winger Alan Hinton crossed for Terry Wharton to head home and things
looked ominous for Town. Nevertheless, with just nine minutes to play Town
almost snatched an equaliser. Digging deep into what energy he had left,
John Elsworthy went on a solo run. At the edge of the penalty area Elsworthy
laid a square pass to Doug Moran whose shot succeeded in sending
Malcolm Finlayson in the Wolves' goal diving the wrong way. Luck was not

with Moran, however, and the ball struck Finlayson's trailing boot. Within two minutes Wolves had sealed the points, as Roy Bailey was unable to hold Wharton's shot and Hinton snapped up the rebound.

The result pushed Town two places down the table to fifth as both West Ham United and Tottenham Hotspur leap-frogged over them. But Burnley lost too, so Town were no further off the pace. Wolverhampton Wanderers were now fifteenth.

Elsewhere in Division One these were the results on 11 November:

Aston Villa	3–1	Arsenal
Blackburn Rovers	2–0	Birmingham City
Blackpool	1–1	Everton
Cardiff City	2–1	Sheffield Wednesday
Chelsea	1–0	Bolton Wanderers
Manchester United	2–2	Leicester City
Nottingham Forest	3–2	Burnley
Sheffield United	3–1	Manchester City
Tottenham Hotspur	4–2	Fulham
West Ham United	2–4	West Bromwich Albion

Match No. 18
Saturday 18 November 1961
Venue: Portman Road
Ipswich Town 4–1 Manchester United   Attendance: 25,755

The visit of Manchester United to Portman Road was yet another first. Town had played United once before, but never in a league game. That one match, an FA Cup fourth round tie in January 1958, was famously United's last game prior to their ill-fated trip to Munich.

United had been in the First Division since last winning promotion in 1938. They had won the Championship three times in the past decade, the last time being in 1957, but they had not won a trophy since and had finished seventh in the table in the previous two seasons.

Despite a lack of silverware in the past few seasons, United's team was still littered with international players; Bobby Charlton, Warren Bradley and Billy Foulkes had all represented England and Nobby Stiles would too, although not until 1965, by which time of course Alf Ramsey would be England manager. In addition Johnny Giles had, and Tony Dunne and Seamus Brennan would, play for Eire.

Roy Stephenson had not recovered from the thigh strain he sustained at Wolverhampton and so Alf Ramsey had to choose between reserves Aled Owen and Dermot Curtis to fill the number seven shirt. It was Curtis who got Alf's vote on the strength of a good performance ten days earlier for the reserves against Northampton Town. It was to be Curtis's thirty-fourth first team game for Town since signing from Bristol City in 1958.

Mr K.G. Aston of Ilford was the referee and the teams lined up as follows – Ipswich Town: Bailey; Carberry and Compton; Baxter, Nelson and Elsworthy; Curtis, Moran, Crawford, Phillips and Leadbetter. Manchester United: Gaskell; Brennan and Dunne; Stiles, Foulkes and Setters; Bradley, Giles, Herd, Charlton and McMillan.

As happened so many times in games against the 'big teams' in Town's first season in the top division, the match was to end in a glorious victory for Town. Yet again the performances of Ray Crawford and Ted Phillips would prove decisive. The England manager Walter Winterbottom was at the game and the headline in the *East Anglian Daily Times* read 'Phillips gives Winterbottom food for thought'.

As thoughtful as he might have been, Mr Winterbottom must also have enjoyed this game, which was hard fought and very exciting. Town took the lead on twenty-five minutes when Ted Phillips thundered a square pass from Ray Crawford into the net from about twenty-five yards out. Despite a great deal of effort from both teams there was no further scoring until the sixty-seventh minute when once again Ray Crawford laid the ball off to Ted Phillips who hit another screaming shot from about twenty-five yards. This time John Gaskell in the United goal dived the wrong way, probably because the ball took a deflection, but possibly to simply get out of its way.

The game now seemed safe but, just to make sure, Ray Crawford added a third. Four minutes from time and John Elsworthy then added his name to the score sheet with a comedy goal. Elsworthy lobbed the ball 'into the mixer' and a mass of Town forwards and United defenders leapt up to head it; this left Gaskell unsighted and when everyone failed to connect with the ball it fell to ground and bounced between Gaskell's legs into the net.

Embarrassed perhaps by the score and the nature of the last goal, United swept forward in the dying minutes of the game and claimed a consolation when Sam McMillan poked the ball home. But for this late effort Town's defence had dominated the United players; Nelson had subdued David Herd, and Bobby Charlton had had a quiet game. Larry Carberry had been magnificent and his full-back partner John Compton had only been beaten once all afternoon, with the result that United's wingers had not troubled Town. The only player to receive any criticism in the *East Anglian*'s report was the reserve wide man Dermot Curtis, who the report said had tended to dwell on the ball a bit too long which had slowed down some of Town's attacking moves.

That Saturday night Ipswich were back up to third in the table with twenty-one points from eighteen games; one point behind Everton and three points behind the leaders Burnley.

The week preceding the game versus Manchester United had seen just one midweek fixture in the remainder of Division One; that result and the others played on Saturday 18 November went as follows:

14 November
Arsenal   1–0   Sheffield Wednesday

18 November
Arsenal   2–1   Nottingham Forest
Birmingham City   4–0   West Ham United
Bolton Wanderers   1–1   Aston Villa
Burnley   3–3   Wolverhampton Wanderers
Everton   1–0   Blackburn Rovers
Fulham   0–1   Blackpool
Leicester City   3–0   Cardiff City
Manchester City   2–2   Chelsea
Sheffield Wednesday   0–0   Tottenham Hotspur
West Bromwich Albion   3–1   Sheffield United

League Cup Third Round
Tuesday 21 November 1961
Venue: Villa Park
Aston Villa 2–3 Ipswich Town   Attendance: 22,000

The teams for this League Cup game were as follows – Aston Villa: Sims; Lee and Aitken; Crow, Sleeuwenhoek and Deakin; McParland, Wylie, Thomson, O'Neill and Burrows. Ipswich Town: Bailey; Carberry and Compton; Baxter, Nelson and Elsworthy; Owen, Moran, Curtis, Phillips and Leadbetter. The referee was Ray Tinkler.

Without both Roy Stephenson and Ray Crawford, who was on international duty, Ipswich could have been forgiven for being a bit more defensive than usual against the League Cup holders. Nevertheless Jimmy Leadbetter gave Town the lead after a quarter of an hour and Ted Phillips doubled the lead with a header twenty minutes later. Two minutes into the second half Villa pulled a goal back through Burrows. Fifteen minutes from time Villa equalised, again through Burrows, but this time with a penalty as a result of a handball by Andy Nelson. Villa's joy lasted only two minutes, however, as another handball, this time by Aitken, gave a spot-kick to Ipswich, which Ted Phillips scored to send Town into the fourth round of the League Cup.

The following day, Wednesday 22 November, was an auspicious day for Ipswich Town and for Ray Crawford in particular as he became the first Town player to be selected to play for the English national team. The game was against Northern Ireland in the Home International Championship and a Wembley crowd of around 30,000 saw a 1–1 draw with Bobby Charlton scoring England's goal but with Ray Crawford providing the 'assist'.

Match No. 19
Saturday 25 November 1961
Venue: Ninian Park
Cardiff City 0–3 Ipswich Town   Attendance: 22,823

The visit to mid-table Cardiff City offered the prospect to Town of another two very winnable points if they could do themselves justice and avoid the sort of below-par performance they had given against a mediocre Blackpool in the previous month. Cardiff City were not a team with much of a First Division pedigree. This was the Bluebirds' third stay in the First Division having most recently been promoted in 1960. Previously, they had spent five seasons in Division One between 1952 and 1957, never finishing higher than tenth, but prior to that they had not been in the top division since the 1920s when they enjoyed their best campaigns. The previous season they had finished fifteenth and while they were currently in mid-table, 1961/62 would prove to be a deeply disappointing one for them, culminating in their relegation from the top division to which they have never returned. Town had previously played Cardiff City in both Division Two and Division Three (South).

Roy Stephenson returned to the team for this match having recovered from the thigh strain he suffered at Molineux a fortnight beforehand. The referee was Mr J. Kelly of Chorley and these were the teams – Cardiff City: John; Harrington and Milne; Hole, Rankmore and Baker; King P., Tapscott, King J., Ward and Hogg. Ipswich Town: Bailey; Carberry and Compton; Baxter, Nelson and Elsworthy; Stephenson, Moran, Crawford, Phillips and Leadbetter

It would seem that Town were in no mood to let Cardiff City off the hook and the *East Anglian Daily Times* reported a comfortable victory referring to Town playing 'deadly, efficient football, polished and planned.' For the first time too, reference was made to the possibility of Town challenging for the league championship as the headline read 'Ipswich sights are set on Championship'.

Town certainly seemed to mean business and took the lead in this match after only eight minutes. Ray Crawford pushed the ball across to Ted Phillips who was some thirty yards from goal and at quite a steep angle to it. Despite the distance and angle, Phillips' swerving shot flew just inside the far post. The goal clearly pleased Ted as the *East Anglian* described him as dancing around in celebration like 'a man demented'.

From there on Town did not look back. Cardiff had more of the possession but when they had the ball Town used it to far greater effect. Doug Moran had an excellent game and could have scored a hat-trick while the defence, and in particular Andy Nelson, were so much in command that Roy Bailey did not have a save to make until the last ten minutes of the game.

Town's second goal arrived with just three minutes to go before half time. Ray Crawford passed the ball from the left to Roy Stephenson who swept the ball on to Ted Phillips, who in turn moved it to Doug Moran; Moran shot and his effort would have beaten John in the Cardiff goal, but Frank Rankmore attempted a clearance and only succeeded in helping the ball over the line.

Town were able to ease up in the second half, as Cardiff seemed to know that they were beaten, although they still created a handful of reasonable chances. But on eighty-four minutes Town scored a third. Roy Stephenson ran from the middle of the pitch out to the left-hand side from where he laid the ball back to Jimmy Leadbetter; he crossed the ball accurately to meet Ted Phillips who was racing in towards goal and scored with a downwards header.

Burnley had won their fixture also, thrashing Manchester United at Old Trafford, so Town remained three points off the top of the table, but they were now in second place for the first time having vaulted over Everton, who had lost at West Ham. The result left Cardiff City in twelfth place.

The table (after the other results that day) looked like this:

	P	W	D	L	F	A	Pts	Goal Ave.
Burnley	18	12	2	4	55	36	26	1.53
Ipswich Town	19	10	3	6	47	35	23	1.34
Everton	19	10	2	7	36	24	22	1.50
West Ham United	19	9	4	6	43	39	22	1.10
Sheffield Wednesday	19	9	3	7	37	26	21	1.42
Tottenham Hotspur	18	9	3	6	30	27	21	1.11
Leicester City	19	9	2	8	36	32	20	1.13
Arsenal	19	7	6	6	33	33	20	1.00
Fulham	19	7	5	7	34	32	19	1.06
Bolton Wanderers	19	8	3	8	30	29	19	1.03
Aston Villa	18	7	4	7	28	28	18	1.00
Cardiff City	19	6	6	7	28	31	18	0.90
Blackpool	19	6	6	7	28	32	18	0.88
West Bromwich Albion	19	5	7	7	34	34	17	1.00
Nottingham Forest	19	6	5	8	30	35	17	0.86
Sheffield United	18	7	3	8	21	33	17	0.64
Wolverhampton Wanderers	19	6	4	9	32	34	16	0.94
Manchester City	19	7	2	10	35	42	16	0.83
Manchester United	18	6	4	8	27	38	16	0.71
Birmingham City	19	6	4	9	30	43	16	0.70
Chelsea	19	5	5	9	36	39	15	0.92
Blackburn Rovers	18	5	5	8	20	28	15	0.71

And here are the results which led to the table on the previous page:

Aston Villa	2–1	Manchester City
Blackburn Rovers	0–2	Fulham
Blackpool	1–3	Sheffield Wednesday
Chelsea	4–1	West Bromwich Albion
Manchester United	1–4	Burnley
Nottingham Forest	0–1	Bolton Wanderers
Sheffield United	3–1	Birmingham City
Tottenham Hotspur	1–2	Leicester City
West Ham United	3–1	Everton
Wolverhampton Wanderers	2–3	Arsenal

Meanwhile . . .

On 1 November the ten-minute 'drinking-up time' rule was introduced in pubs. This gave pub-goers a little more time to take their minds off the scares circulating this month about radioactive fall-out from recent Soviet nuclear tests. Hopefully there would be no fall-out at Sizewell where construction was under way of the nuclear power station. But at least it was going to be easier to use the telephone as subscriber Standard Trunk Dialling was introduced to Ipswich, meaning that you no longer had to go through the operator to have a call connected. Also in Ipswich, but five days later, on 6 November, Thurleston Secondary School on Defoe Road was opened; this was the first new school in Ipswich to be opened since 1939. The youth of Whitton have never looked back.

If you wanted to bunk off school for the afternoon, Walt Disney was providing cartoon entertainment in the shape of *101 Dalmations* at the Gaumont, while the ABC was showing the comedy *What a Carve Up!*

On Friday 3 November the nation rejoiced at an addition to the Civil List with the birth of Princess Margaret's first child. The following evening Helen Shapiro appeared live on stage at the Gaumont. This was perfect timing for young Helen who was top of the hit parade at the time, but only until 9 October when Elvis Presley took over with a double 'A' side of 'Little Sister' and 'His Latest Flame'. Elvis remained at number one for the rest of the month.

Other events occurring during the month included the continuing trial of James Hanratty for the murder of Michael Gregsten and rape of Valerie Storey at Deadman's Hill on the A6 in August 1961. More grim news included the murder of a policeman in a machine gun attack at the Eire/Ulster border in south Armagh.

Earlier in the month Her Majesty the Queen had left Britain to visit Ghana, while on 17 November President Charles De Gaulle was in London for talks with Harold MacMillan, the prime minister of the day.

On 29 November the USA sent Enos, a five-and-a-half-year-old chimpanzee, into space where it was expected he would spend about four-and-a-half hours orbiting the Earth three times. In practice however, he came back to Earth after just two orbits.

Football news included Jimmy Hill's decision on 6 November to retire from playing football due to a persistent knee injury. But Jimmy was back in the news on 29 November when he became manager of Fourth Division Coventry City. There was concern at the offices of the Football League because attendances at matches had declined by over five million since the start of the previous season. The League were to spend between five and ten thousand pounds trying to find out why.

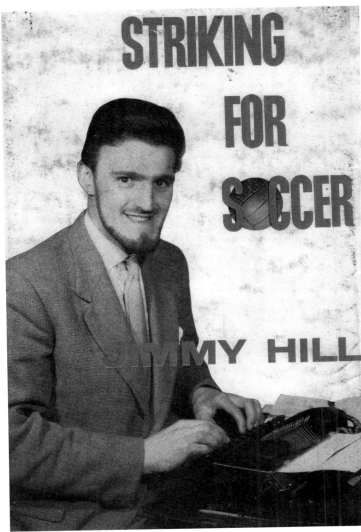

Apart from Ipswich Town's unique and astonishing First Division championship win, the 1961/62 season was also memorable as being the first after the abolition of the maximum wage. Jimmy Hill was the man responsible for this having rallied the Professional Footballers' Association to threaten strike action. He wrote a book to tell the story. (Jimmy Hill, Striking for Soccer, The Sportsmans Book Club, 1963)

December

Match No. 20
Saturday 2 December 1961
Venue: Portman Road
Ipswich 5–2 Chelsea   Attendance: 22,726

With the season approaching the half-way mark Town continued to come up against clubs they had never previously encountered in competitive matches. Next up was Chelsea, a side with a lengthy First Division pedigree, although they had seldom been one of the country's leading teams. Chelsea had been in Division One continuously since 1930, though in all those twenty-four seasons they had only finished in the top half four times. It was more common for them to appear among the bottom five teams and therefore their Championship success in 1955 had been something of a surprise to everyone. In 1961 Chelsea had finished twelfth.

Chelsea had been struggling so far in the 1961/62 season and had been at the bottom of the table. They had just struck a vein of good form, however, as they approached the Ipswich game. Chelsea had sacked manager Ted Drake in September but player/coach Tommy Docherty had led them to a haul of eight points from their last five games, with their most recent success being a 4–1 victory over West Bromwich Albion at Stamford Bridge.

The Chelsea side contained four future England internationals in Peter Bonetti, Ken Shellito, Bobby Tambling and Barry Bridges, but they were due to earn only fifteen caps between them. At full-back they were also to field Ron 'Chopper' Harris. The referee was Mr P. Bye and these were the teams – Ipswich Town: Bailey; Carberry and Compton; Baxter, Nelson and Elsworthy; Stephenson, Moran, Crawford, Phillips and Leadbetter. Chelsea: Bonetti; Shellito and Harris; Malcolm, Scott and Bradbury; Murray, Tambling, Brabrook, Bridges and Blundstone.

This was yet another thoroughly entertaining match for the Portman Road crowd with a deluge of goals. Chelsea belied their lowly position in the league table giving as good as they got, and were the better side at times. The difference once again, however, between Town and their opponents, was their striking ability and on this particular occasion it was the ability of Ray Crawford. The headline on the *East Anglian Daily Times* sports pages read 'Ray Crawford's hat-trick sinks Chelsea'.

Crawford had got Town off to a flying start with a goal from Roy Stephenson's pass after just four minutes. But Chelsea came back almost immediately with Bobby Tambling collecting a pass from Bridges before shooting past Bailey to equalise. Parity was to last only until the fifteenth minute when Ted Phillips had what was oddly enough his only decent shot of the game. Even then Phillips did not score, but typically the force of Phillips' shot meant Bonetti could only parry the ball and Doug Moran accepted the gift of a simple tap-in. For the next half an hour up until half time Town were forced on to the back foot as Chelsea dominated, going in search of another equaliser. Indeed, Town were fortunate to stay ahead as Brabrook's shot hit a post and bounced along the goal line.

As the second half started home supporters must have worried about whether Town could hold on, but their fears were soon eased when in the fifty-second minute Roy Stephenson sent over a cross that Ray Crawford met with a precise header to make the score 3–1. But still Chelsea were not beaten and after sixty-six minutes Brabrook and Blundstone exchanged passes to set up Murray who reduced the deficit to a single goal again.

It was a very even game and Chelsea impressed with fast, intricate and accurate passing. However, Andy Nelson was outstanding at the heart of the Town defence and with Chelsea constantly frustrated, Town now went on to score twice more. First, in the seventy-fourth minute Ray Crawford claimed his hat-trick, shooting through a crowded penalty area to score. Then, Roy Stephenson went on a run, finally taking a shot at goal that Bonetti saved only for the ball to return to Stephenson who scored with his second attempt.

Ipswich could be said to have been a shade fortunate to win this match, and by such a scoreline too. Chelsea were certainly unlucky, but Town had defended superbly when necessary and when the opportunity to strike back came they took their chances; the result kept Town in second place in the table behind Burnley who had also won, at home to Sheffield United who had been promoted with Town the previous April.

These were the day's other results in Division One:

Arsenal	2–2	West Ham United
Birmingham City	3–0	Cardiff City
Bolton Wanderers	1–1	Blackburn Rovers
Burnley	4–2	Sheffield United
Everton	5–1	Manchester United
Fulham	0–1	Wolverhampton Wanderers
Leicester City	0–2	Aston Villa
Manchester City	2–4	Blackpool
Sheffield Wednesday	3–0	Nottingham Forest
West Bromwich Albion	2–4	Tottenham Hotspur

Match No. 21
Saturday 9 December 1961
Venue: Villa Park
Aston Villa 3–0 Ipswich Town   Attendance: 31,924

The half-way stage of the season brought Town up against yet another side against whom they had never played a league game. Town had played Villa in a League Cup tie, however, just a few weeks before, running out 3–2 winners. The only encounter with Villa prior to that had been in the third round of the FA Cup back in January 1939 when Ipswich were in their first season in the Football League. Back then a glorious 1–1 draw at Villa Park was followed up with a narrow 2–1 defeat at Portman Road.

Aston Villa were the side with the longest First Division pedigree of any club. Since becoming founder members of the Football League in 1888 they had spent only three seasons outside the top division, fewer than any other club. They had won six league championships, albeit all before the First World War. Villa's most recent excursion into Division Two, however, which had been for a single season, was very recent indeed, with their having been Second Division Champions in 1960, just a year before Town. Villa were now managed by Joe Mercer who had won three league championship medals as a player and would go on to manage Manchester City to the league championship in 1966.

On the day before the game the only doubt for Town was whether or not the Army would grant leave to conscript Billy Baxter as he was due to take part in a rehearsal for a parade at Aldershot on the Saturday. In the event Baxter was able to play.

The referee for the afternoon's game was Mr F. Cowan of Manchester and the two teams lined up as follows – Aston Villa: Sims; Lee and Atkinson; Crowe, Sleeuwenhoek and Deakin; MacEwan, Thomson, Dougan, Wylie and McParland. Ipswich Town: Bailey; Carberry and Compton; Baxter, Nelson and Elsworthy; Stephenson, Moran, Crawford, Phillips and Leadbetter.

The result of this match was very disappointing for Town, particularly as they expected better having won their last three games and reduced the points gap between themselves and Burnley. Aston Villa must be given credit, however, for they were exceptionally good on the day and more than made up for their home defeat to Town in the League Cup.

Town started the game reasonably enough and having survived some early Villa attacks they played some good football of their own, though they failed to trouble Nigel Sims in the Villa goal. But they did not build up any momentum and began to be pushed back by Villa before they eventually gave way under the pressure. The opening goal came from Northern Ireland international and Villa stalwart Peter McParland who scored after Larry Carberry had been caught out of position and Roy Bailey had been slow to come off his line.

Villa had to wait until the forty-seventh minute to extend their lead but again a defensive error by Town was to blame. This time Larry Carberry miskicked and it was McParland who benefited for a second time. Bob Thomson completed the scoring after eighty-two minutes after already missing a chance from just three yards out. Villa could easily have had more goals as McParland hit the crossbar and both Carberry and John Compton made goal-line clearances.

Late on Jimmy Leadbetter missed the chance to score a consolation goal for Town after a Ted Phillips header had hit the crossbar and rebounded to him; but for that Town made little impression.

Part of Town's undoing had been the rampant form of Peter McParland who had tormented Larry Carberry who, for his part, had received little protection from Jimmy Leadbetter in front of him. Also significant was the clash between Derek Dougan, another Northern Ireland international, and Andy Nelson, which the Irishman had just edged. On top of losing the defensive battle, Town had been unable to provide decent service to Ray Crawford and Crowe had got the better of Ted Phillips. It was no wonder that Town had lost the game.

This seventh defeat of the season left Town five points behind Burnley who had won at Chelsea. Town also dropped a place in the table behind Everton for whom a single point from a draw at Cardiff had been enough to lift them up into second place. The day's results in Division One are listed in full below:

Blackburn Rovers	4–1	Manchester City
Blackpool	2–2	West Bromwich Albion
Cardiff City	0–0	Everton
Chelsea	1–2	Burnley
Manchester United	3–0	Fulham
Nottingham Forest	0–0	Leicester City
Sheffield United	2–1	Arsenal
Tottenham Hotspur	3–1	Birmingham City
West Ham United	1–0	Bolton Wanderers
Wolverhampton Wanderers	3–0	Sheffield Wednesday

For Ipswich Town, their first historic season in the First Division of the Football League was now half over. They had played most teams at least once with only Arsenal and Leicester City not having visited Portman Road or having played host to the Town. A small clutch of just six clubs had only played twenty matches, two of those being title favourites Burnley and Tottenham Hotspur who were both clearly well in the running for the title.

On the evening of Saturday 9 December the full league table now looked like this:

	P	W	D	L	F	A	Pts	Goal Ave.
Burnley	20	14	2	4	61	39	30	1.56
Everton	21	11	3	7	41	25	25	1.64
Ipswich Town	21	11	3	7	52	40	25	1.30
Tottenham Hotspur	20	11	3	6	37	30	25	1.23
West Ham United	21	10	5	6	46	41	25	1.12
Sheffield Wednesday	21	10	3	8	40	29	23	1.38
Aston Villa	20	9	4	7	33	28	22	1.18
Leicester City	21	9	3	9	36	34	21	1.06
Arsenal	21	7	7	7	36	37	21	0.97
Blackpool	21	7	7	7	34	36	21	0.94
Wolverhampton Wanderers	21	8	4	9	36	34	20	1.06
Bolton Wanderers	21	8	4	9	31	31	20	1.00
Fulham	21	7	5	9	34	36	19	0.94
Cardiff City	21	6	7	8	28	34	19	0.82
Sheffield United	20	8	3	9	25	38	19	0.66
West Bromwich Albion	21	5	8	8	38	40	18	0.95
Blackburn Rovers	20	6	6	8	25	30	18	0.83
Nottingham Forest	21	6	6	9	30	38	18	0.79
Birmingham City	21	7	4	10	34	46	18	0.74
Manchester United	20	7	4	9	31	43	18	0.72
Manchester City	21	7	2	12	38	50	16	0.76
Chelsea	21	5	5	11	39	46	15	0.85

League Cup Fourth Round

Monday 11 December 1961
Venue: Ewood Park
Blackburn Rovers 4–1 Ipswich Town   Attendance: 11,071

The teams for this match lined up as follows: Blackburn Rovers: Else; Taylor and Newton; Clayton, Woods and McGrath; Douglas, Lawther, Pickering, Byrom and Ratcliffe. Ipswich Town: Bailey; Carberry and Compton; Baxter, Nelson and Elsworthy; Stephenson, Moran, Crawford, Phillips and Leadbetter. The evening's referee was Mr V. James.

This was a game in which Town were well beaten, as the scoreline attests. Blackburn went ahead on twenty-three minutes through Lawther but by half time Town were level through a fortieth-minute Ted Phillips penalty, incidentally Phillips' only shot of the game. Blackburn had to wait until the sixty-eighth minute to regain the lead when seventeen-year-old John Byrom scored. Thereafter, Blackburn scored twice more, firstly on seventy-five minutes when Pickering converted a penalty and then on eighty-one minutes when Pickering completed the scoring.

Match No. 22
Saturday 16 December 1961
Venue: Portman Road
Ipswich Town 2–1 Bolton Wanderers   Attendance: 16,587

Twelfth-placed Bolton Wanderers became the fourth side (after Burnley, Blackburn and Fulham) that Town had played twice, as the season moved into its second half and the fixtures on the opening day of the season were reversed. Bolton Wanderers manager Bill Ridding made two changes from the side that had drawn 0–0 with Town at Burnden Park back in August; Jack Threlfall replaced half-back Roy Wilkinson, and at centre forward he selected Ernie Phythian. Northern Ireland international Billy McAdams, who had played up front in the first fixture, had since been sold to Second Division Leeds United.

Roy Bailey played his 250th game for Town in this fixture. While Ken Malcolm had returned to fitness, having captained the reserves at Shrewsbury during the week, he failed to dislodge John Compton from the Town team.

This afternoon's referee was Mr W. Clements of West Bromwich and the teams lined up like this – Ipswich Town: Bailey; Carberry and Compton; Baxter, Nelson and Elsworthy; Stephenson, Moran, Crawford, Phillips and Leadbetter. Bolton Wanderers: Hopkinson; Hartle and Farrimond; Threlfall, Edwards and Rimmer; Holden, Stevens, Phythian, Hill and Pilkington.

Like Chelsea in the previous home fixture, Bolton Wanderers travelled to Portman Road having hit a rich vein of form. The Trotters had conceded just four goals in their last eight games and now had twenty points, five fewer than Town, who had conceded eleven goals in their past eight games.

It turned out to be a game that for a long time appeared to be one Town would lose. They started well enough, but Wanderers took the lead after thirty-seven minutes through former England international Bert Holden. Brian Pilkington took a corner and with Roy Bailey unsighted, Holden steered the ball through the packed penalty area into the net. Thereafter Bolton proceeded to pack their defence and play with a siege mentality; fouling and wasting time and being generally unpleasant. Town were unsettled by these strong-arm 'tactics' that enraged the home crowd (as, incidentally, they would thirty-eight years later in a promotion play-off match between the two clubs) who were incensed by a series of rough challenges by Wanderers' nineteen-year-old full-back Syd Farrimond on Roy Stephenson. But the less than sporting play from Bolton worked against them in the longer term as the crowd got behind Town and roared them on to victory.

Nevertheless, Town had to wait until the last ten minutes of the match to rescue the points and even then relied on some good fortune. On eighty-three minutes Roy Stephenson took a corner, which the Trotters' goalkeeper Ted Hopkinson caught; but he seemed to be pushed over the goal line by Ray Crawford. The referee immediately awarded a goal despite the protests of the entire Bolton team who claimed, not that Hopkinson had been fouled, but that the ball had not crossed the line; Hopkinson had held on to it.

It seemed that Town had rescued a point and they had seven minutes left to score a second goal. Bolton however, had not conceded more than a single goal in any game since 14 October, some two months earlier.

Town pressed forward with the home crowd giving them loud encouragement, and with two minutes left they scored again. Doug Moran hit a powerful shot which struck Hopkinson's thigh; with no one else reacting as quickly to the loose ball, Ray Crawford nipped between two defenders to slot it home. On the Monday morning the *East Anglian Daily Times* described it rather wonderfully as 'good triumphing over evil.'

The win pushed Town back into second place, just three points behind Burnley who had surprisingly lost at home to Arsenal. Everton, previously in second place, had drawn away from home for a second week running. The full results for the day in Division One were as follows:

Aston Villa	1–1	Everton
Burnley	0–2	Arsenal
Cardiff City	1–1	Blackburn Rovers
Fulham	0–1	Birmingham City
Leicester City	2–0	Manchester City
Manchester United	1–2	West Ham United
Nottingham Forest	3–0	Chelsea
Sheffield Wednesday	2–1	West Bromwich Albion
Tottenham Hotspur	5–2	Blackpool
Wolverhampton Wanderers	0–1	Sheffield United

Match No. 23
Saturday 23 December 1961
Venue: Maine Road
Manchester City 3–0 Ipswich Town   Attendance: 18,376

With Christmas just two days away Town travelled to Maine Road, Manchester, for yet another groundbreaking fixture. Indeed Town could have done with a little groundbreaking, literally, as the match took place on a rock-hard, frosty pitch. Manchester City were languishing in the lower reaches of the division and Town should have been confident of victory against a side that had not won in eight games. The referee was Mr R. Langdale of Darlington and the teams were as follows – Manchester City: Trautmann; Betts and Sear; Cheetham, Leivers and Kennedy; Young, Hannah, Dobing, Hayes and Wagstaffe. Ipswich Town: Bailey; Carberry and Compton; Baxter, Nelson and Elsworthy; Stephenson, Moran, Crawford, Phillips and Leadbetter.

Though it was a game Town perhaps should, on paper, have won, in the end they were well beaten and even lucky to return home having conceded just three goals. The *East Anglian Daily Times* reporter suggested that maybe they were beaten by the frosty surface as much as by Manchester City, but he also conceded that City, although they did not play particularly well, simply seemed to want to win more than Town did.

The first two goals, both in the first half, were down to defensive lapses. Firstly Roy Bailey misjudged a daisy cutter of a shot from the edge of the penalty box by Joe Hayes, letting it just inside the post. For goal number two, the defence left Peter Dobing completely unmarked allowing him to head home a corner taken by Dave Wagstaffe. Such a soft goal was symptomatic of a game in which Andy Nelson was uncharacteristically poor and John Elsworthy appeared to struggle with the conditions. After his mistake on giving away the first goal, Roy Bailey recovered and Billy Baxter and John Compton were the pick of a generally weak defensive performance.

City wrapped the game up within two minutes of the restart as seventeen-year-old Neil Young went on a fabulous run and shot at goal; his initial strike hit Billy Baxter but he managed to despatch the rebound into the net. With the game effectively lost, Town started to play better. Ray Crawford was the best forward on view for either side and twice he forced Bert Trautmann in the City goal to make fine saves. Doug Moran and Roy Stephenson also played well on the right-hand side, but both saw too little of the ball to make a real impression on the game. On the down side Ted Phillips had another quiet game and seemed to be in a poor run of form, and Jimmy Leadbetter was hampered by a strained knee.

The defeat saw Town slide three places down the table into fifth position, their lowest placing in more than a month. Elsewhere in the Division Sheffield United and Nottingham Forest had played on the Friday night and West Ham had met Wolverhampton on the previous Monday. The week's full results were as follows:

18 December

West Ham United	4–2	Wolverhampton Wanderers

22 December

Sheffield United	2–0	Nottingham Forest

23 December

Arsenal	2–1	Tottenham Hotspur
Birmingham City	1–1	Sheffield Wednesday
Blackpool	3–0	Cardiff City
Chelsea	1–0	Aston Villa
Everton	3–0	Fulham
West Bromwich Albion	2–0	Leicester City

Match No. 24
Tuesday 26 December 1961
Venue: Portman Road
Ipswich Town 1–0 Leicester City   Attendance: 18,146

Boxing Day brought the visit to Portman Road of mid-table Leicester City, yet another side against whom the Town had never played a competitive fixture. The Filberts had won the Second Division Championship in 1957 and this was now their fifth consecutive season in Division One. Having been relegated in 1939 they had spent every season since the Second World War in the Second Division except for 1954/55 when they had a one-season excursion into the First Division, at exactly the same time as Town were having a one-season holiday from Division Three (South) in Division Two.

The knee strain that Jimmy Leadbetter had suffered in the 3–0 defeat at Manchester City the previous Saturday meant that he missed this game: it was the first time in 156 matches that he had not appeared for the Town. Leadbetter's replacement was Welshman Aled Owen and it was to be Owen's only league appearance this season. The referee for this match was Mr A. Holland of Barnsley and these were the teams – Ipswich Town: Bailey; Carberry and Compton; Baxter, Nelson and Elsworthy; Stephenson, Moran, Crawford, Phillips and Owen. Leicester City: Banks; Clamers and Norman; McLintock, King and Keyworth; Riley, Walsh, Cheesebrough, Appleton and Mitten. The pitch was once again very hard, but it was also very level so the bounce was an even one. Nevertheless this was not a classic game by any stretch of the imagination and possibly Leicester City deserved a draw.

The first half was goalless although Ted Phillips had a shot deflected narrowly over the crossbar, and for Leicester Jim Walsh went close to scoring, as did John Mitten, twice. Frank McLintock was particularly good for Leicester and almost scored, and Mitten and Howard Riley were a danger to Town due to their pace, but Billy Baxter was strong in the tackle and didn't shirk a challenge and Elsworthy did well too. Town's attack was less effective with Roy Stephenson having a poor game and Aled Owen failing to lift his crosses sufficiently. In the middle Moran and Crawford were not on form and the *East Anglian* reporter described Ted Phillips as being 'in the midst of a deep depression.' Indeed, Phillips had scored just one goal, a penalty, in his last seven appearances. Neither goalkeeper had much to do on this afternoon.

The game had looked like turning out to be a goalless draw until the sixty-seventh minute when Ray Crawford struck. Roy Stephenson had sent an accurate pass out to Aled Owen on the left; Owen's first cross had been blocked but he managed to get the ball over at the second attempt and Ray

Crawford met the cross, hooking the ball wide of Gordon Banks for what would prove to be the only goal of the game.

After that, Leicester looked most likely to score, with Larry Carberry having to clear off the goal line from a Walsh header after a corner. But the Town defence held firm with Andy Nelson being the cornerstone.

The result pushed Town back up into fourth place in the league table but all the teams above them won also. These were the other results in Division One on Boxing Day 1961:

Arsenal	1–0	Fulham
Birmingham City	1–1	Manchester City
Burnley	4–0	Sheffield Wednesday
Cardiff City	1–0	Aston Villa
Chelsea	0–2	Tottenham Hotspur
Everton	1–0	Bolton Wanderers
Manchester United	6–3	Nottingham Forest
Sheffield United	2–1	Blackpool
West Bromwich Albion	1–1	Wolverhampton Wanderers
West Ham United	2–3	Blackburn Rovers

After playing Leicester City at Portman Road on Boxing Day, Town's next scheduled fixture was the return game at Filbert Street on 30 December. However, the Leicester pitch was frozen and there was then a fall of snow on top of it so referee Ken Collinge of Altrincham called the match off after a 9.30 a.m. pitch inspection. The Town party had set off from Ipswich station at 7.55, but word of the cancellation had got to them in time to avoid their having to complete the journey to Leicester. The only game in Division One to survive the weather was the London derby at White Hart Lane between Championship-chasing Tottenham and relegation-threatened Chelsea; this was the result:

Tottenham Hotspur	5–2	Chelsea

This final league fixture of 1961 left the Division One table looking like this as everyone prepared for the arrival of 1962.

	P	W	D	L	F	A	Pts	Goal Ave.
Burnley	22	15	2	5	65	41	32	1.59
Tottenham Hotspur	24	14	3	7	50	36	31	1.39
Everton	24	13	4	7	46	26	30	1.77
Ipswich Town	24	13	3	8	55	44	29	1.25
West Ham United	24	12	5	7	54	47	29	1.15
Arsenal	24	10	7	7	41	38	27	1.08
Sheffield Wednesday	24	11	4	9	43	35	26	1.23
Sheffield United	23	11	3	9	30	39	25	0.77
Aston Villa	23	9	5	9	34	31	23	1.10
Leicester City	24	10	3	11	38	37	23	1.03
Blackpool	24	8	7	9	40	43	23	0.93
Cardiff City	24	7	8	9	30	38	22	0.79
Birmingham City	24	8	6	10	37	48	22	0.77
West Bromwich Albion	24	6	9	9	42	43	21	0.98
Wolverhampton Wanderers	24	8	5	11	39	40	21	0.98
Blackburn Rovers	22	7	7	8	29	33	21	0.88
Bolton Wanderers	23	8	4	11	32	34	20	0.94
Nottingham Forest	24	7	6	11	36	46	20	0.78
Manchester United	22	8	4	10	38	48	20	0.79
Fulham	24	7	5	12	34	41	19	0.83
Manchester City	24	8	3	13	42	53	19	0.79
Chelsea	25	6	5	14	42	56	17	0.75

Meanwhile . . .

At the Gaumont cinema in Ipswich *The Guns of Navarone* was showing, while at the ABC/Ritz in the Buttermarket the entertainment was considerably lighter with the screening of *What A Whopper*, a comedy about the Loch Ness monster. Moving on to Christmas, the pantomime at the Ipswich Theatre in Tower Street was *Cinderella*, a very apposite choice given Ipswich Town's arrival in the First Division as the 'Cinderella' club.

Frankie Vaughan was the first artist to claim top spot in the hit parade in December as he replaced Elvis Presley on 7 December singing something called 'Tower of Strength', which was destined to be the Christmas number one for 1961. Frankie stayed at the top of the chart for three weeks but was finally toppled on 28 December by Andy Williams singing 'Moon River'. Perhaps the most widely remembered record of the time, however, was Acker Bilk's 'Stranger on the Shore', an instrumental number which entered the chart in November, reached the number two position and featured in the chart for fifty-five weeks.

In sport other than football, on 5 December Henry Cooper was knocked out by Zora Folley after just one minute and eight seconds of their bout at the Empire Pool, Wembley.

Away from the world of sport and games, on 11 December thirty-four Ban the Bomb protestors were imprisoned for making their feelings known at the NATO base at Wethersfield, two days beforehand. Elsewhere there was talk of raising the school leaving age to sixteen and in the House of Commons there was angry debate over the proposed Commonwealth Immigration Bill.

Further from home, on 15 December in Jerusalem wartime Nazi Adolf Eichmann was sentenced to death for war crimes. Even further away, Indian forces were sent to Goa amid fears of invasion by the Portuguese! Not to be outdone, Britain was also mobilising its forces, with naval ships sailing north from Mombasa towards Aden as 'a precautionary measure'. In Baghdad, where the people in charge were also claiming they should run Kuwait, this action by Britain was denounced as a 'plot against Iraq'.

With the arrival of Christmas the weather became much colder. Temperatures dropped below freezing on Boxing Day as Britain fell into the grip of a 'Big Freeze'. By the turn of the year the Automobile Association was moved to say 'Britain is like a vast iceberg.' As well as freezing weather, Christmas also heralded a work to rule by Post Office employees.

But the cold weather must have suited near-neighbours Colchester United because on 30 December they rattled up their record victory as they despatched hapless Bradford City, thrashing the Bantams 9–1.

January 1962

The first Saturday of January is traditionally set aside for the third round of the FA Cup and 6 January 1962 was no exception. Ipswich had been drawn at home to Second Division Luton Town. Despite bad weather in the preceding week the game went ahead, albeit on a slushy pitch.

FA Cup Third Round
Saturday 6 January 1962
Venue: Portman Road
Ipswich Town 1–1 Luton Town   Attendance: 18,450

The teams lined up as follows – Ipswich Town: Bailey; Carberry and Compton; Baxter, Nelson and Elsworthy; Stephenson, Moran, Crawford, Phillips and Owen. Luton Town: Baynham; McNally and Bramwell; Morton, Cope and Pacey; Walden, Ashworth, Chandler, McKechnie and Legate. The referee was Mr K. Dagnall of Bolton.

Luton, eleventh in Division Two, brought about 1,000 fans with them for this fixture although they had returned a number of unsold seat tickets. Fortunately for Town they scored in the very first minute through Ted Phillips, who headed in a cross from Roy Stephenson. They were fortunate because otherwise they played poorly, never managing to match the enthusiasm and pace of Luton. Ted Phillips had a particularly poor game.

Luton scored the equaliser they deserved after fifty-seven minutes when Robin Chandler converted a cross from Alec Ashworth. Luton could, and possibly should, have won the game, but they had a blatant penalty appeal rejected by referee Mr Dagnall who perhaps fancied a trip to Luton the following Wednesday evening for the replay.

FA Cup Third Round Replay
Wednesday 10 January 1962
Venue: Kenilworth Road
Luton Town 1–1 Ipswich Town (aet)   Attendance: 23,818

Ipswich had not known until the Monday whether Bill Baxter would get leave from the Army to be available to play; as it happened he was, but Jimmy Leadbetter was still out and Aled Owen again wore the number eleven shirt.

These were the teams – Ipswich Town: Bailey; Carberry and Compton; Baxter, Nelson and Elsworthy; Stephenson, Moran, Crawford, Phillips and Owen. Luton Town: Baynham; McNally and Bramwell; Morton, Cope and Pacey; Walden, Ashworth, Chandler, McKechnie and Legate. Once again Mr Dagnall was the referee.

This was a much more entertaining game than the first tie and Ipswich played a lot better, particularly in defence. Once again Ipswich scored first, this time after sixteen minutes when John Elsworthy hit a twenty-yard shot after a corner had been only partly cleared. It took Luton until fourteen minutes from time to equalise when the aptly named Dave Pacey chased a through-ball from McKechnie and then cracked in a shot off the under side of the crossbar. Thirty minutes extra time ensued but no further goals were scored.

The Football Association and the police were far better organised back in the 1960s and so teams could have as many replays as they liked and there was no such thing as a penalty shoot-out. This meant that Ipswich and Luton would have the pleasure of a second replay, at a neutral ground.

Match No. 25
Saturday 13 January 1962
Venue: Portman Road
Ipswich Town 3–0 West Bromwich Albion   Attendance: 18,378

The cancellation of the game on 30 December, and the fact that there was no New Year's Day Bank Holiday back in 1961, gave Town a second consecutive home fixture. But it also meant that Town had not played a league fixture for almost three weeks, although they had met Luton Town in the FA Cup a week before hand and in a replay just three days before. The FA Cup tie was still not settled and needed to go to a second replay at a neutral venue, Highbury, just two days after this fixture.

The extended lay-off from the league programme had allowed Jimmy Leadbetter time to recover from his knee strain and so he replaced Aled Owen in Town's line-up. The teams were – Ipswich Town: Bailey; Carberry and Compton; Baxter, Nelson and Elsworthy; Stephenson, Moran, Crawford, Phillips and Leadbetter. West Bromwich Albion: Wallace; Howe and Williams S.; Robson, Jones and Drury; Jackson, Burnside, Smith, Kevan and Clark. The referee for this fixture was dear old Mr Fussey of Retford, who had officiated in a match earlier in the season.

This was a game that, in contrast to recent matches, Town won well, and deservedly so. Roy Bailey was quite busy in goal early on but as the game wore on West Brom's forwards had few ideas and troubled him less and less. Bailey was well protected by his defenders however, with Billy Baxter shackling the potential match-winner and England international Derek Kevan, scorer of 150 career goals for the Albion. John Elsworthy also had the measure of another England international, Bobby Robson, and Andy Nelson was completely dominant in the centre of defence.

Don Howe, another England player, usually started Albion's attacks and they performed well enough in midfield, but their attacks broke down from thereon. For Town, Roy Stephenson was particularly good and it was he who scored the first goal after just sixteen minutes with a low shot into the far corner from a narrow angle.

Town did not score again until five minutes into the second half when once again Roy Stephenson played a part, running forty yards with the ball before putting Doug Moran through to shoot hard past Wallace. Jimmy Leadbetter completed the scoring in the final minute with a goal very similar to the opening one from Roy Stephenson.

It was an entertaining game in which Doug Moran was singled out for praise for his excellent performance. Ted Phillips had a much-improved game after his recent disappointments and Ray Crawford came very close to scoring with a shot that hit the crossbar. Jimmy Leadbetter was said to have had the miss of his career having hit the ball over the bar from just two yards.

The result moved Town another place up the league table into third; two points behind Tottenham Hotspur on thirty-three and three behind leaders Burnley. The day's other Division One results went like this:

Arsenal	1–2	Bolton Wanderers
Aston Villa	0–0	Sheffield United
Burnley	6–3	Manchester City
Cardiff City	1–1	Tottenham Hotspur
Fulham	3–4	Chelsea
Leicester City	1–2	Birmingham City

Manchester United	0–1	Blackpool
Nottingham Forest	3–0	West Ham United
Sheffield Wednesday	3–1	Everton
Wolverhampton Wanderers	0–2	Blackburn Rovers

There was one midweek league fixture on the following Monday, 15 January:

Manchester United	2–0	Aston Villa

But the same night Ipswich Town were also in action, although not in the league, as they once again tried to overcome Luton Town to reach the fourth round of the FA Cup.

FA Cup Third Round Second Replay
Monday 15 January 1962
Venue: Highbury
Ipswich Town 5–1 Luton Town   Attendance: 29,438

The choice of neutral venue for this game, Highbury, was a good one, as would have been most London grounds. Incredibly the attendance for this match was greater than for either of the two previous ties; there must have been many neutrals at the game, which shows the appetite for FA Cup football among the public at the time and indicates that football was still easily affordable.

For the third game in this tie Jimmy Leadbetter was back in the Ipswich team, but Roy Bailey was out and was replaced by Wilf Hall. Luton Town manager Sam Bartram also made a change to his side, replacing Cope with Kelly in the half-back line. The two teams therefore lined up like this – Ipswich Town: Hall; Carberry and Compton; Baxter, Nelson and Elsworthy; Stephenson, Moran, Crawford, Phillips and Leadbetter. Luton Town: Baynham; McNally and Bramwell; Morton, Kelly and Pacey; Walden, Ashworth, Chandler, McKechnie and Legate. The referee for this match was Mr R.H. Mann of Worcester.

The result of this match was arguably settled before it kicked off as Luton captain Morton won the toss but opted to play into the strong wind. Ipswich took the lead in the first minute when Doug Moran scored from eight yards following a Ted Phillips throw-in. Five minutes later Crawford passed to Stephenson who ran forward and crossed to Leadbetter who tapped the ball through to Ted Phillips to score with a hard left-foot shot. After a further ten minutes Leadbetter went to go around Mcnally, but was chopped down, allowing Ted Phillips to make the score 3–0 from the penalty spot.

Luton Town tried to get back into the game in the second half and on fifty-six minutes Alec Ashworth headed in after McNally had shot. Luton pushed on from this but Town held firm in defence and Luton eventually ran out of steam allowing Roy Stephenson to net twice more in the final ten minutes. The win meant Ipswich now had an away tie at Carrow Road.

Match No. 26
Saturday 20 January 1962
Venue: St Andrews
Birmingham City 3–1 Ipswich Town   Attendance: 26,968

Town had humbled Birmingham City by four goals to one back at Portman Road in September and Birmingham were destined for a fairly humble final place in the league table come the end of the season – seventeenth. But on this afternoon Town and Birmingham swapped identities and the headline in the *East Anglian* the following Monday morning read, 'Ipswich surrender long before the end at St Andrews'.

While Town fielded a side with just one change from that which had beaten Birmingham so well in September, the City team showed six changes. For Town, Wilf Hall replaced Roy Bailey who had tonsillitis. For Birmingham City, John Schofield replaced Withers in goal, and full-backs Lynn and Sissons came in for Foster and Allen (yes, they were really called Foster and Allen). Half-back Terry Hennessey, who was to win a league championship medal with Derby County in 1972, replaced Watts, and in the forward line Welsh international Ken Leek (yes, a Welshman called Leek) replaced Taylor, and Bertie Auld, a future European Cup winner with Celtic in 1967, replaced Brian Singer. This same line-up had played in Birmingham's previous match, a 2–1 win at Filbert Street, Leicester. The referee for this afternoon's game was Mr S. Pickles of Stockport. The teams were – Birmingham City: Schofield; Lynn and Sissons; Hennessey, Smith and Beard; Hellawell, Bloomfield, Harris, Leek and Auld. Ipswich Town: Hall; Carberry and Compton; Baxter, Nelson and Elsworthy; Stephenson, Moran, Crawford, Phillips and Leadbetter.

This match was one that Town could and perhaps should have won. Birmingham City were not an impressive side by any means and indeed they produced no worthwhile chances in the whole of the second half. But Town's forwards were lacklustre and wasted the clear chances that came their way; often being too elaborate in their play. In the first half Leadbetter, Moran and Crawford might all have scored. There can have been few excuses for Town on a day when the conditions were good and the playing surface was one of the best they had encountered all season.

The first goal came after just ten minutes when City broke quickly from a Town free-kick, taken about twenty yards from the City goal. Sissons cleared the ball to Bertie Auld who sent Leek through the centre of the Town defence to score.

Six minutes later Leek doubled his and Birmingham's tally with a fine shot on the turn which Wilf Hall could not be faulted for letting in. Birmingham's final goal came in the fiftieth minute courtesy of Billy Baxter and Wilf Hall. Baxter had intercepted a through-ball but he then hurriedly passed it back to Wilf Hall, not seeing that Hall was some ten yards off his line. Although he reacted and dived, the ball went past Hall into the net.

Just three minutes later Town were given the opportunity to get back into the game when, after another poor back-pass, Ray Crawford tapped the ball in from just a couple of yards. But the goal failed to raise Town from their slumber and the game was lost, pushing them back down to fourth position in the league table behind Everton and Tottenham, and Burnley who had drawn 1–1 at West Bromwich Albion. With their two games in hand Burnley could potentially be eight points ahead of Town, but of course they had to win those games.

No further league matches were played in January, with the FA Cup fourth round taking place the following Saturday. The first month of 1962 therefore ended with the Division One table looking like this:

	P	W	D	L	F	A	Pts	Goal Ave.
Burnley	24	16	3	5	72	45	35	1.60
Tottenham Hotspur	26	14	5	7	53	39	33	1.36
Everton	26	14	4	8	50	31	32	1.61
Ipswich Town	26	14	3	9	59	47	31	1.26
West Ham United	26	13	5	8	56	50	31	1.12
Sheffield Wednesday	26	13	4	9	48	36	30	1.33
Sheffield United	25	12	4	9	33	40	28	0.83
Blackpool	26	10	7	9	48	45	27	1.07
Arsenal	26	10	7	9	44	43	27	1.02
Birmingham City	26	10	6	10	42	50	26	0.84
Blackburn Rovers	24	9	7	8	33	34	25	0.97
Aston Villa	26	9	6	11	34	35	24	0.97
Cardiff City	26	7	10	9	32	40	24	0.80
Leicester City	26	10	3	13	41	42	23	0.98
Bolton Wanderers	25	9	5	11	35	36	23	0.97
Manchester United	25	9	5	11	42	51	23	0.82
West Bromwich Albion	26	6	10	10	43	47	22	0.91
Nottingham Forest	26	8	6	12	40	48	22	0.83
Wolverhampton Wanderers	26	8	5	13	41	49	21	0.84
Manchester City	26	9	3	14	48	61	21	0.79
Fulham	26	7	5	14	37	47	19	0.79
Chelsea	27	7	5	15	47	62	19	0.76

The other matches in the Division One programme to produce the table on the opposite page were:

Blackburn Rovers	2–1	Nottingham Forest
Blackpool	7–2	Wolverhampton Wanderers
Bolton Wanderers	1–1	Cardiff City
Everton	3–2	Leicester City
Fulham	0–2	Sheffield Wednesday
Manchester City	3–2	Arsenal
Sheffield United	3–1	Chelsea
Tottenham Hotspur	2–2	Manchester United
West Bromwich Albion	1–1	Burnley
West Ham United	2–0	Aston Villa

Returning to the FA Cup fourth round, Town had been drawn against Norwich City at Carrow Road. Back in the 1960s Carrow Road was a far bigger ground than Portman Road, having quite large terraces on three sides of the pitch. A crowd bigger than any ever seen at Portman Road witnessed the game.

FA Cup Fourth Round
Saturday 27 January 1962
Venue: Carrow Road
Norwich City 1–1 Ipswich Town   Attendance: 39, 890

As you might expect, this game was eagerly awaited. Norwich, who were twelfth in Division Two, fielded a team that was radically different from the one that had lost their previous fixture, a home game versus mighty Rotherham United, with seven changes, five of them in defence. The teams were as follows – Norwich City: Kennon; Thurlow and Ashman; McGoham, Butler and Mullett; Mannion, Allcock, Conway, Hill and Lythgoe. Ipswich Town: Hall; Carberry and Compton; Baxter, Nelson and Elsworthy; Stephenson, Moran, Crawford, Phillips and Leadbetter. The referee was Mr Ken Aston of Ilford.

In spite of the keen anticipation, this game turned out to be a flop, possibly the worst ever local derby between Ipswich and Norwich. There was no score at half time, but three minutes into the second half Norwich took the lead as Allcock beat Andy Nelson in the air to head home. The lead lasted only five minutes, however, as Larry Carberry played the ball to Doug Moran who touched it on for Jimmy Leadbetter to skip around Thurlow and shoot past Kennon.

The replay was set for Portman Road the following Tuesday evening.

FA Cup Fourth Round Replay
Tuesday 31 January 1962
Venue: Portman Road
Ipswich Town 1–2 Norwich City   Attendance: 29,796

Despite it having been such a dire game on the Saturday, the respective team managers stuck with the same teams for the replay. Happily they produced a much better game in spite of a frozen and therefore slippery pitch.

It was a game dominated by Ipswich who had a good three-quarters of the possession and enjoyed a corner count of twelve to one in their favour. For all their dominance, however, Town trailed at half time to a fortieth-minute lob-cum-volley from Allcock.

But it only took four minutes of the second half for Town to equalise, as Jimmy Leadbetter's corner kick bounced down to Ray Crawford who hooked the ball into the net. Doug Moran then hit the crossbar, but that possibly gave the clue that it wasn't to be Town's night. With just two minutes remaining Mannion beat John Compton on the flank and crossed hard for Allcock to side-foot home the winning goal. This was surely the biggest disappointment of the season, but I think I'd settle for losing at home to Norwich in the cup if it meant winning the league title.

Meanwhile . . .
The beginning of January had been very cold indeed. In places it had been too cold for people to work; aeroplanes had frozen to the ground and there had been extremely dense fog. The worst of this most wintry weather had been south of a line running roughly from the River Humber to Anglesey.

But in Ipswich the population could forget about the weather because of the fine entertainment at the cinema. At the Gaumont Elvis Presley was starring in *GI Blues* for people who liked that kind of thing, but also playing was *The Angry Silence* starring Richard Attenborough. Shot in black and white, the film was part of the new wave of realism in British films telling unglamorous stories about the lives of ordinary working-class people. The significant thing for Ipswich cinema-goers about this particular film was that it had been filmed in the town at Reavell's factory in Ranelagh Road.

Also on at the Gaumont during January was *Room at the Top*, one of the most famous and earliest of the new wave of British films. By January 1962 this X-rated film was hardly a new release, being about three years old and it wasn't filmed in Ipswich. At the ABC/Ritz cinema in the Buttermarket there was another film that was to become a classic; *Breakfast at Tiffany's* starring Audrey Hepburn.

Aside from the excellent films on offer it was an exciting month in other parts of the town too. On Friday 12 January, half-way through the Bingo game at the Co-op social club in Crabbe Street, there was a police raid!

It seems it was the result of an infringement of club regulations. The *East Anglian Daily Times* also reported on 23 January that two Ipswich lads, 'dressed in tight trousers and black jackets,' were fined £10 by Ipswich magistrates. The report didn't make it wholly clear what they had done, so perhaps they were just inappropriately dressed.

A story that might have been big but ultimately proved a damp squib was the recommendation of Ipswich by the Town and Country Planning Association as one of five English towns to be used for the decentralisation of London office accommodation. Apart from the arrival of Willis Faber & Dumas and Guardian Royal Exchange in the 1970s, this of course never really materialised.

Away from Ipswich the Ford Motor Company launched the Ford Capri on 3 January with a starting price of £915. Ford described it as their first ever 'personal car' which I guess meant it wasn't a family saloon.

On 11 January there was a new number one in the hit parade as Cliff Richard and the Shadows went straight to the top with 'The Young Ones' and they stayed at number one for the remainder of the month and virtually all of February too.

There was a health scare in the north and the Midlands with a number of reported cases of smallpox. This even caused three matches involving Bradford City and Bradford Park Avenue to be postponed and Town had had to consider whether or not to travel to Birmingham for their match on 20 January.

Finally, back to a purely football story which was the appointment of Tommy Docherty as Chelsea manager in place of Ted Drake who had departed Stamford Bridge back in November.

February

Match No. 27
Saturday 3 February 1962
Venue: Portman Road
Ipswich Town 4–2 Everton   Attendance: 22,572

After the disappointment of losing at Birmingham City a fortnight before, and the even bigger shame of going out of the cup to Norwich, at home, Town needed to bounce back to recapture the momentum of their season. The visit of Everton, who were a place above Town in the table, therefore presented very tough opposition indeed. But yet again Town would produce some of their best football for one of the biggest matches, against a top team. The headline in the *East Anglian* on the following Monday read, 'swept off their feet'.

In the run-up to the game there had been murmurings that Alf Ramsey might drop Ted Phillips from the side due to his poor form of late, but in the end the Town team was unchanged from the one that had lost at St Andrews except for the return of Roy Bailey, who had of course recovered from his bout of tonsillitis in time for the FA Cup match at Norwich the weekend before. Harry Catterick's Everton showed four changes from the side that had beaten Town 5–2 at Goodison Park in September. Youngster Colin Green had replaced George Thomson at full-back, while up front Alex Young, Derek Temple and Jimmy Fell had lost their places to Bobby Collins, Roy Vernon and Michael Lill.

The referee was Mr H. Horner of Coventry and the teams lined up like this – Ipswich Town: Bailey; Carberry and Compton; Baxter, Nelson and Elsworthy; Stephenson, Moran, Crawford, Phillips and Leadbetter. Everton: Dunlop; Parker and Green; Gabriel, Labone and Harris; Bingham, Collins, Young, Vernon and Lill.

The decision not to drop Ted Phillips was vindicated after just six minutes when he scored the opening goal. The lead lasted for another eighteen minutes until Northern Ireland international Billy Bingham equalised, having exchanged passes with Vernon. But Town succeeded in re-establishing, and then extending, their lead before half time. Firstly, Doug Moran scored with a fine header from a Roy Stephenson corner that eluded the Everton defence. Then, on forty-two minutes Roy Stephenson was fouled. From the resultant free-kick he crossed for John Elsworthy to score his second, and last, goal of the 1961/62 league campaign.

Town completed their scoring just thirteen minutes into the second half. Phillips went on a long run before passing to Jimmy Leadbetter who then crossed for Ray Crawford to shoot and score from a very narrow angle. Town's three-goal lead remained intact until the very end of the game when Harris chalked up a late consolation goal from a powerful drive.

It was a good performance from Town and in particular winger Roy Stephenson, whose dominance of the inexperienced Everton full-back Colin Green was significant. But in addition Ray Crawford played well and Ted Phillips had been involved in most of Town's attacking moves. Elsewhere on the field John Elsworthy had been a force in the middle and John Compton had kept winger Billy Bingham subdued.

The victory took Town into second place in the table, above their defeated opponents Everton, and Tottenham Hotspur who lost at Wolverhampton. Burnley still led the Championship race however, and consolidated their position by thrashing Birmingham City at Turf Moor. Perhaps most significantly, although no one could possibly have realised it at the time, this was the start of a sixteen-match run for Town which would see them lose only one more match before end of the season.

The weekend's other Division One results were as follows:

Arsenal	0–1	West Bromwich Albion
Aston Villa	1–0	Blackburn Rovers
Bolton Wanderers	0–2	Manchester City

Burnley	7–1	Birmingham City
Chelsea	0–1	West Ham United
Leicester City	4–1	Fulham
Manchester United	3–0	Cardiff City
Nottingham Forest	3–4	Blackpool
Sheffield Wednesday	1–2	Sheffield United
Wolverhampton Wanderers	3–1	Tottenham Hotspur

Match No. 28
Saturday 10 February 1962
Venue: Craven Cottage
Fulham 1–2 Ipswich Town   Attendance: 25,209

The visit to Craven Cottage presented Town with the opportunity to avenge what had been their last home league defeat, back in late September. Since then they had won nine consecutive league fixtures. Fulham were ripe for the picking, having lost their previous eight games. The Cottagers were fourteen points behind Town, having accumulated nineteen points from the twenty-seven games they had played so far. Their points had been gathered from seven wins and five draws, with the other fifteen games naturally enough having been lost.

Bedford Jezzard's Fulham team showed five changes from the team that had won at Portman Road five months earlier. Langley, O'Connell, Chamberlain and Key were out and Mealand, Leggatt, Henderson and Metchik were in, while Tony Macedo the keeper had a sprained wrist and was replaced by Hawkins. Town fielded their usual eleven, although this represented a change from the previous encounter with Fulham when Wilf Hall had stood in for the injured Roy Bailey. The full line-ups were – Fulham: Hawkins; Chen and Mealand; Mullery, Dodgin and Lowe; Crook, Leggatt, Henderson, Haynes and Metchik. Ipswich Town: Bailey; Carberry and Compton; Baxter, Nelson and Elsworthy; Stephenson, Moran, Crawford, Phillips and Leadbetter. The referee for this game was Mr R.J. Leafs of Nottingham.

After the sound performance that saw Town beat close rivals Everton, this was a disappointing effort from the Town, but they nevertheless ran out comfortable winners. Fulham were probably hampered by some of their players not being fully fit. Both Haynes and Leggatt had heavily bandaged thighs and, perhaps as a result, Haynes always remained in a deep position and did not trouble the Town rearguard as he had done back in September.

Fulham's best player, and probably the best player from either side, was future England international Alan Mullery. It was Mullery who, after thirteen minutes and against the run of play, gave Fulham the lead with a fine goal at the end of a twenty-yard run.

Despite trailing, Town were the better organised of the two teams with Ray Crawford looking sharp and Roy Stephenson clearly having the better of his marker, full-back Mealand. Thirteen minutes after Mullery's goal, Town equalised as Roy Stephenson sent over a high cross, and stand-in goalie Hawkins, without any challenge, simply punched the ball into his own net.

Despite their superiority, Town were not playing well enough to kill this game off and had to wait until the seventy-eighth minute before scoring the goal that would claim both points. Again Roy Stephenson was the provider as he exchanged passes with Doug Moran before hitting a cross-field ball to Ray Crawford who scored.

But for the result, the game had been disappointing from Town's perspective. Roy Bailey had played his part in the win, saving well from Cook and Henderson, but Ted Phillips had struggled to find any form and the usually inspiring John Elsworthy was not at his best either.

Despite the win Town slipped back to third in the table as Tottenham Hotspur had beaten Nottingham Forest 4–2 and so had a superior goal average. Town were, however, a point closer to Burnley at the top, as they had only managed to draw at Everton. The top of Division One now looked like this:

	P	W	D	L	F	A	Pts
Burnley	26	17	4	5	81	48	38
Tottenham Hotspur	28	15	5	8	58	44	35
Ipswich Town	28	16	3	9	65	50	35
Everton	28	14	5	9	54	37	33
West Ham United	28	14	5	9	58	32	33

The other Division One results for the weekend were as follows, with Cardiff having played on the Friday night:

9 February
Cardiff City	2–3	Wolverhampton Wanderers

10 February
Birmingham City	1–0	Arsenal
Blackburn Rovers	3–0	Chelsea
Blackpool	1–2	Aston Villa
Everton	2–2	Burnley
Manchester City	0–2	Manchester United
Sheffield Wednesday	1–2	Leicester City
Tottenham Hotspur	4–2	Nottingham Forest
West Bromwich Albion	6–2	Bolton Wanderers
West Ham United	1–2	Sheffield United

The following weekend only four fixtures were played in Division One, with Chelsea playing on the Friday night and the other three matches kicking off on the Saturday. These were the results of those games:

16 February
Chelsea   1–0   Blackpool

17 February
Bolton Wanderers   3–2   Birmingham City
Leicester City   2–2   West Ham United
Nottingham Forest   2–1   Cardiff City

Without a league fixture themselves, Ipswich Town chose to play a friendly in order to 'keep their hand in', as it were.

Friendly
Saturday 17 February 1962
Venue: Portman Road
Ipswich Town 5–0 TSV Alemannia Aachen   Attendance: 10,765

The teams for this friendly were – Ipswich Town: Bailey; Carberry and Compton; Baxter, Nelson and Pickett; Stephenson, Moran, Crawford, Phillips and Leadbetter. TSV Alemannia Aachen: Schors; Krisp and Nievelstein; Mayer, Willms and Krämer; Stein, Martinelli, Bergstein, Glenski and Zebec. The referee was Mr J.R. Osborne from Ipswich.

Town rested John Elsworthy, and Reg Pickett took his place in the side. The Germans were poor, but they were only part-time professionals and they provided no real test for Ipswich who ran out easy winners. Town were 3–0 up by half time thanks to Ray Crawford (twice) and Roy Stephenson. Crawford completed his hat-trick after seventy-four minutes and Roy Stephenson rounded off the scoring three minutes later.

Before the next set of Saturday fixtures a number of First Division teams had rearranged matches to play midweek; these were the results:

20 February
Burnley   2–1   Fulham
Sheffield United   0–0   Blackburn Rovers

21 February
Aston Villa   0–0   Tottenham Hotspur
Manchester City   3–1   West Bromwich Albion

Match No. 29
Saturday 24 February 1962
Venue: Upton Park
West Ham United 2–2 Ipswich Town   Attendance: 27,763

When Town had played West Ham earlier in the season the Hammers had been second in the table and Town sixth. Both clubs had maintained their form in the intervening matches and, much like Town, West Ham United had made few alterations to their team. For this game Edward Bovington replaced Geoff Hurst, and Ronnie Boyce came in for Phil Woosnam. Both Bovington and Boyce only ever played League football for the Hammers. The referee for this return game was Mr P.G. Brandwood of Wolverhampton who had also officiated in the first game back in October at Portman Road. The teams were – Ipswich Town: Bailey; Carberry and Compton; Baxter, Nelson and Elsworthy; Stephenson, Moran, Crawford, Phillips and Leadbetter. West Ham United: Leslie; Kirkup and Bond; Bovington, Brown and Moore; Scott, Boyce, Sealey, Dick and Musgrove.

This was a thrilling match, albeit one played on a very hard and bumpy pitch. Town were probably marginally the better side and might have been worth the win. Scottish international goalkeeper Lawrie Leslie had a good game for West Ham but Town had only themselves to blame for not collecting both points, as they gifted the Hammers both of their goals.

First blood was drawn by West Ham on seven minutes courtesy of former Hammer Andy Nelson, whose weak and poorly directed clearance fell to John Dick who was happy to send the ball back from ten yards into the net.

After twenty minutes Roy Stephenson took a corner from the right for which Ray Crawford and Lawrie Leslie both jumped. The ball fell to Jimmy Leadbetter who avoided Joe Kirkup in forcing the ball over the line for the equaliser.

Town were playing as well as they had in any away match since the early part of the season. Doug Moran worked ceaselessly and Ray Crawford might have scored, but Kirkup took the ball off his toe as he was about to shoot; Andy Nelson was battling well with Dick and Sealey, and Billy Baxter was turning in a man of the match-type performance. It was Baxter indeed who saved Town from going behind a second time before the interval as he athletically cleared off the goal line, and ended up in the net himself, after Dick's shot had beaten Roy Bailey.

Within two minutes of the start of the second half, however, Town did fall behind. This time it was Roy Bailey's turn to make the Hammers happy. Joe Kirkup shot from distance and Bailey had it covered; he got to the ball easily but then let it spin from his grasp and it rolled into the net.

Six minutes later Town might have equalised from Doug Moran's effort but for a linesman's flag, which ruled out the goal due to an offside.

Nevertheless, eventually, twelve minutes from time, Town got the reward their efforts deserved. Winger Malcolm Musgrove, back defending, handled a shot from Jimmy Leadbetter. Lawrie Leslie would probably have saved Leadbetter's shot, but he was not so fortunate with the penalty kick from Ted Phillips, who, despite having a mediocre game, scored his thirtieth goal of the season.

On the stroke of full time Billy Baxter went on a solo run into the West Ham penalty area and Edward Bovington appeared to handle the ball. Referee Mr Brandwood thought otherwise, however, and no penalty was given and so the game ended all square.

So February came to an end with Town still challenging at the top of the table. They were still trailing a few points behind leaders Burnley, who also had games in hand and were obvious favourites to lift the title. Town were in the company of a clutch of clubs all trailing in the wake of Burnley and all potentially on hand to claim the title should the Lancashire club falter.

The result kept Town in third place but they had closed in on second-placed Spurs, who had only drawn at home to Bolton Wanderers, and the leaders Burnley who had been beaten 2–1 in the local derby at Ewood Park, Blackburn.

The other results in Division One that day went like this:

Aston Villa	2–0	Fulham
Blackburn Rovers	2–1	Burnley
Blackpool	0–1	Arsenal
Cardiff City	0–0	Manchester City
Chelsea	1–0	Sheffield Wednesday
Manchester United	4–1	West Bromwich Albion
Nottingham Forest	2–1	Everton
Sheffield United	3–1	Leicester City
Tottenham Hotspur	2–2	Bolton Wanderers
Wolverhampton Wanderers	2–1	Birmingham City

One midweek match was played but it had no bearing on the top positions in the table:

28 February
Wolverhampton Wanderers	2–2	Manchester United

The final table for the month of February 1962 therefore ended up looking like this:

	P	W	D	L	F	A	Pts	Goal Ave.
Burnley	28	18	4	6	84	51	40	1.65
Tottenham Hotspur	30	15	7	8	60	46	37	1.30
Ipswich Town	29	16	4	9	67	52	36	1.29
West Ham United	30	14	7	9	62	56	35	1.11
Sheffield United	29	15	5	9	40	43	35	0.93
Everton	29	14	5	10	55	39	33	1.41
Aston Villa	30	12	7	11	39	36	31	1.08
Sheffield Wednesday	29	13	4	12	50	41	30	1.22
Blackburn Rovers	28	11	8	9	38	36	30	1.06
Manchester United	29	12	6	11	53	54	30	0.98
Blackpool	30	11	7	12	53	52	29	1.02
Arsenal	29	11	7	11	45	45	29	1.00
Leicester City	30	12	4	14	50	49	28	1.02
Wolverhampton Wanderers	30	11	6	13	51	55	28	0.92
Birmingham City	30	11	6	13	47	62	28	0.76
West Bromwich Albion	30	8	10	12	52	56	26	0.93
Bolton Wanderers	29	10	6	13	42	48	26	0.88
Nottingham Forest	30	10	6	14	49	58	26	0.84
Manchester City	30	11	4	15	53	64	26	0.83
Cardiff City	30	7	11	12	35	48	25	0.73
Chelsea	31	9	5	17	49	66	23	0.74
Fulham	30	7	5	18	40	57	19	0.70

Meanwhile . . .

Back in the real world there was plenty going on both in Britain and the rest of the world with events taking place that would be remembered in years to come and end up on the GCSE history syllabus.

On 3 February the United States government took the decision to ban imports from Cuba, as they cranked up the Cold War a little bit more. Nine days later one of the biggest stories of the era came to the fore with the release by the USSR of United States Air Force pilot Francis Gary Powers. Powers' U2 plane had been brought down by the Russians on 1 May 1960 as he flew over Soviet territory. Had he been spying, or had he just got a little lost?

The Americans thumbed their noses yet again at the Commies on 20 February when they announced that Major John H. Glenn had successfully orbited the earth three times in his Mercury capsule, *Friendship Seven*. The Americans had not yet 'invaded' Vietnam but it was in the news too as Communist planes bombed Saigon on the same day.

Back in Blighty three million shipbuilding and engineering workers went on strike on 5 February. On 17 February the longest murder trial in British history came to its conclusion after twenty-one days. James Henratty was found guilty and sentenced to death.

22 February saw a change in the world of popular music as Elvis Presley dislodged Cliff Richard and the Shadows from the top of the hit parade. Elvis usurped Cliff with a double 'A' side of 'Rock-a-Hula Baby' and 'Falling in Love'.

Returning to Ipswich, things were far less grisly, although that might have been a matter of opinion as on 24 February the Gaumont played host to Cliff Richard. At the Ipswich cinemas during February there was lashings of action and drama with *The Day the Earth Caught Fire* at the Odeon, *Ben Hur* at the ABC and *On the Waterfront* at the Gaumont.

Finally, returning to football, near-neighbours Colchester United were blazing a trail five points clear at the top of Division Four.

March

Match No. 30
Saturday 3 March 1962
Venue: Portman Road
Ipswich Town 4–0 Sheffield United   Attendance: 20,158

After games against two of their nearest challengers (Everton and West Ham) in recent weeks, Town were now due to meet yet another of the division's high fliers with the visit to Portman Road of fifth-placed Sheffield United. The Blades had been runners-up to Town in last season's Second Division title race and with just two points less than Town this season, and a game in hand, were performing as much above expectations as Town were. In fact, their recent form was better than Town's as they were undefeated in their last sixteen league and Cup games.

The only change for United, compared to the side that had beaten Town at Bramall Lane in October, was the inclusion of Keith Kettleborough in place of Ron Simpson, although there was also some shuffling of positions among the team. These were the line-ups: Ipswich Town – Bailey; Carberry and Compton; Baxter, Nelson and Elsworthy; Stephenson, Moran, Crawford, Phillips and Leadbetter. Sheffield United: Hodgkinson; Coldwell and Shaw G.; Richardson, Shaw J. and Summers; Allchurch, Kettleborough, Pace, Russell and Hartle. The referee was Mr E.T. Jennings of Stourbridge.

Yet again, despite the opposition's billing as a 'contender' Town were to run out as comfortable winners. The headline in the *East Anglian Daily Times* read 'Sheffield United give up record without a fight' and the report commented that the game was in fact no more of a contest than Town's recent friendly against TSV Alemannia Aachen that Town had won 5–0. The only sour note in the report was the reflection that 'the disintegration of Ted

Phillips is more or less complete' and that he was effectively carried by his team-mates in this game. Despite his thirty goals this season Ted Phillips had been singled out in several recent *East Anglian* match reports as having played poorly.

In contrast to Phillips, Ray Crawford was described as the consummate England forward, and his mastery of United's centre-half Joe Shaw was the foundation for the victory. At the back Andy Nelson was imperious and Larry Carberry and John Compton eliminated any threat from the Sheffield United wingers. Town attacked Sheffield from all angles and areas and this proved to be an easy game. So carried away was the *East Anglian*'s reporter that he asked the question, 'Do Burnley have enough in hand to be able to hold off the challenge of the Town for the Championship?'

Town's first goal came after ten minutes when Roy Stephenson ran in from the wing to the middle of the pitch, drawing the Sheffield defence out. Stephenson then played a through-ball that Doug Moran spotted, ran on to and scored. A quarter of an hour later Roy Stephenson set Town on the way to doubling their lead after being brought down on the edge of the penalty area; he crossed and after a bout of head tennis between Doug Moran and Ray Crawford, Jimmy Leadbetter forced his way through to score the second.

The second half belonged to Ray Crawford as he bamboozled the Sheffield United defence with numerous swerving and feinting runs and he added two more goals in the fifty-eighth and seventy-fifth minutes.

The win pushed Town back up to second place in the table, a position that they were destined not to fall below for the remainder of the season. Burnley had now just one game in hand over Town, but had added considerably to their goal average by hammering West Ham United and they now led Town by four points.

	P	W	D	L	F	A	Pts
Burnley	29	19	4	6	90	51	42
Ipswich Town	30	17	4	9	71	52	38
Tottenham Hotspur	31	15	7	9	62	52	37

These were the other results for Saturday 3 March:

Arsenal	0–0	Blackburn Rovers
Birmingham City	1–1	Manchester United
Bolton Wanderers	0–0	Blackpool
Burnley	6–0	West Ham United
Everton	4–0	Wolves
Fulham	1–1	Nottingham Forest
Manchester City	6–2	Tottenham Hotspur
Sheffield Wednesday	3–0	Aston Villa
West Bromwich Albion	5–1	Cardiff City

Match No. 31
Friday 9 March 1962
Venue: Portman Road
Ipswich Town 2–1 Sheffield Wednesday   Attendance: 23,713

This was a rearranged game that had been due to be played on Saturday 17 February, but Sheffield Wednesday were then still in the FA Cup. Wednesday had lost their cup tie to Manchester United after a replay and were therefore now available to play, on what was another FA Cup weekend. Town went into this home clash six points ahead of their opponents. Like Town, The Owls had only drawn four matches but they had lost three more games and won three fewer. Wednesday manager Vic Buckingham fielded a team that showed three changes from the side that Town had beaten at Hillsborough the previous September. McAnearney (who was out for the season after a knee operation), Craig and Ellis were replaced by Robin Hardy, Colin Dobson and Gerry Young; the latter would in three years time win a solitary England cap. Ipswich Town: Bailey; Carberry and Compton; Baxter, Nelson and Elsworthy; Stephenson, Moran, Crawford, Phillips and Leadbetter. Sheffield Wednesday: Springett; Johnson and Megson; Hardy, Swan and Kay; Wilkinson, Dobson, Young, Fantham and Finney. The referee for this match was Mr C.A.R. Woan of Reading.

Wednesday opened the scoring after just six minutes. Fantham and Finney exchanged passes down the left-hand side of the field before Dobson flicked the resultant cross behind Roy Bailey with a deft header. After this the pace of the game increased, with Ted Phillips playing especially well and Andy Nelson outshining Peter Swan, his England international counterpart on the Wednesday team. Wednesday's England international goalkeeper Ron Springett frustrated Town, however. Springett was always cool, assured and quick to act, as he did when saving well from a Ray Crawford header and from a stinging Ted Phillips shot.

Town had to wait until the twenty-ninth minute for their equaliser. Out on the right wing Roy Stephenson first went inside and then outside the full-back Don Megson (Gary Megson's father incidentally) before crossing low to Ray Crawford who scored.

Victory in this match came very late, courtesy again of Roy Stephenson. It was the eighty-sixth minute when Stephenson sped between two defenders onto an overhead kick from Ray Crawford before lashing the ball into the net. Arguably Peter Swan was at fault for the goal as he could possibly have headed the ball clear. It is perhaps ironic that this should be so as Swan would later be accused of throwing Wednesday's game at Ipswich in the 1962/63 season after he, Tony Kay and David Layne had placed bets on Wednesday to lose, which they did. All three were sentenced to four months in prison.

The win had a shadow cast over it, however, by what was thought to be a serious injury to Billy Baxter. The *East Anglian's* match report the next day went under the headline 'Baxter has suspected broken bone in his leg'. With Town's next game being the visit to third-placed Tottenham Hotspur this was exactly what Town did not need.

Neither Burnley nor Tottenham Hotspur played in the league this weekend as both were still in the FA Cup; Town therefore, were able to take advantage, closing the gap on Burnley and moving further ahead of Spurs.

	P	W	D	L	F	A	Pts
Burnley	29	19	4	6	90	51	42
Ipswich Town	31	18	4	9	73	53	40
Tottenham Hotspur	31	15	7	9	62	52	37

These were the other results in Division One that weekend:

Friday 9 March
Chelsea   1–1   Birmingham City

Saturday 10 March
Blackpool   2–1   Leicester City
Nottingham Forest   1–2   Manchester City
Wolverhampton Wanderers   5–1   Bolton Wanderers

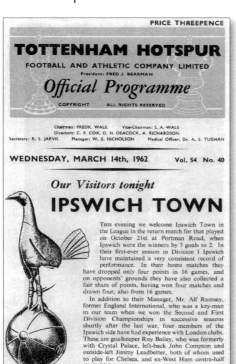

PRICE THREEPENCE

TOTTENHAM HOTSPUR
FOOTBALL AND ATHLETIC COMPANY LIMITED
President: FRED J. BEARMAN

Official Programme

COPYRIGHT   ALL RIGHTS RESERVED

Chairman: FREDK. WALE   Vice-Chairman: S. A. WALE
Directors: C. F. COX, D. H. DEACOCK, A. RICHARDSON
Secretary: R. S. JARVIS   Manager: W. E. NICHOLSON   Medical Officer: Dr. A. E. TUGHAN

WEDNESDAY, MARCH 14th, 1962   Vol. 54 No. 40

Our Visitors tonight

IPSWICH TOWN

THIS evening we welcome Ipswich Town in the League in the return match for that played on October 21st at Portman Road, when Ipswich were the winners by 3 goals to 2. In their first-ever season in Division 1 Ipswich have maintained a very consistent record of performance. In their home matches they have dropped only four points in 16 games, and on opponents' grounds they have also collected a fair share of points, having won four matches and drawn four, also from 16 games.

In addition to their Manager, Mr. Alf Ramsey, former England International, who was a key-man in our team when we won the Second and First Division Championships in successive seasons shortly after the last war, four members of the Ipswich side have had experience with London clubs. These are goalkeeper Roy Bailey, who was formerly with Crystal Palace, left-back John Compton and outside-left Jimmy Leadbetter, both of whom used to play for Chelsea, and ex-West Ham centre-half Andy Nelson.

League titles are of course won over a whole season's fixtures and the points gained from one game are of no more importance than those gained from any other. However, the away fixture at White Hart Lane might be said to have been portentous. With the season entering its final six weeks, Town became the only team to do the 'double' over the previous season's double winners in front of the largest crowd to watch them that season. Alf Ramsey described it as 'the best victory in the history of the club.'

Match No. 32
Wednesday 14 March 1962
Venue: White Hart Lane
Tottenham Hotspur 1–3 Ipswich Town   Attendance: 51,098

Approaching this hugely important game for both clubs, Town received some good news. Billy Baxter's leg was only severely bruised and not broken; there was even a chance he would be fit to face Tottenham. But there was another potential problem to overcome with regard to Baxter, however, as he was due to play for the Army at Dover and he would need special permission to miss that game in order to play for Ipswich. Happily that permission was granted and Baxter was also fit enough to play. Ray Crawford also received some good news when he was selected to play in a representative eleven for the League against the Scottish League at Villa Park on 21 March. Inclusion in the League XI was just a step away from being selected for England.

For their part, Tottenham had just won their way into the FA Cup semi-finals with a 2–0 win at Villa Park. In addition, Spurs were preparing for their two-legged European Cup semi-final tie with Benfica, having beaten Dukla Prague the week before. Spurs had lost just once at home all season, to Leicester.

Included in the Tottenham team was Jimmy Greaves who had recently returned to England for a fat fee after a brief spell playing in Italy for AC Milan. Greaves' inclusion, in place of Les Allen (father of Clive and Bradley who were to become League footballers themselves), was the only change from the Spurs team that had lost at Portman Road back in October of 1961.

Many Town fans made the trip to White Hart Lane for this vital game. Special trains went from Ipswich to Northumberland Park station with a return fare of 13s 6d. The largest crowd for any Town game throughout the season witnessed this match and these were the teams they saw – Tottenham Hotspur: Brown; Baker and Henry; Blanchflower, Norman and McKay; Medwin, White, Smith, Greaves and Jones. Ipswich Town: Bailey; Carberry and Compton; Baxter, Nelson and Elsworthy; Stephenson, Moran, Crawford, Phillips and Leadbetter. The referee was Mr W.E. Haynes of Leicester.

Once again, in common with every other Town match against top opposition in this season, this was a fabulous spectacle. Town took the lead after only eight minutes when Ray Crawford beat Maurice Norman and ran through to shoot past Brown in the Spurs goal. But within minutes Jimmy Greaves had levelled the scores as he ran on to a precise through-ball from Danny Blanchflower and planted the ball past Roy Bailey. The game was now on and Tottenham applied increasing pressure, but Bailey was in superb form while John Elsworthy and Andy Nelson stood firm, seemingly snuffing out any threat from Bobby Smith altogether.

Town were an equally useful attacking force, however, and on twenty-six minutes Ray Crawford ran in from the left leaving Norman and Baker trailing in his wake. Crawford sent in a low, hard centre and Roy Stephenson met it first time; the ball crashed against a post and rebounded to Ted Phillips who again turned it back to Roy Stephenson. Stephenson's shot sailed high over the crossbar. There was no let-up in the action. On forty minutes Medwin appeared to have been brought down but with the home crowd baying for a penalty, the referee waved play on. Within a minute Norman attempted to clear the Tottenham lines but did not do so accurately. The ball fell to Roy Stephenson who proceeded down the right-hand side before floating in a chipped cross towards Ted Phillips who leapt high above two Spurs defenders to head the ball just inside the post past a motionless Bill Brown.

Into the second half and the game continued with action at both ends. John Compton twice cleared the ball off the Town goal line while Bill Brown had to make two attempts at keeping out a Ray Crawford shot. Bill Baxter and Jimmy Greaves battled with one another but Baxter probably just about had the upper hand. Ipswich constantly looked dangerous in attack but still Greaves shot wide from a lobbed Blanchflower pass and Baxter cleared off the goal line from Henry. Doug Moran shot a foot wide of the goal from Crawford's pass and Ted Phillips stung Bill Brown's hands from long range.

Then, with barely twenty minutes left Ray Crawford prised an opening in the Spurs defence through which he let in Ted Phillips to score from a narrow angle and seal the game for Town. Unusually for a Phillips goal, the shot was accurately placed rather than blasted. Still the result was not a certainty as Baxter blocked a MacKay shot that seemed certain to register, and Elsworthy and Carberry also kept out Spurs' goal attempts. But as Spurs became increasingly desperate to score so they looked less likely to. Doug Moran came closer to extending Town's lead with a chip that Brown tipped onto the crossbar with less than ten minutes to go. But still there was time for Spurs to waste a free-kick after Greaves was brought down on the edge of the box, and finally in the last minute Doug Moran put the ball into the Tottenham net, only for it to be ruled out for an offside.

This was a hugely important result at a vital time of the season and it was achieved in a most brilliant game. The *East Anglian Daily Times'* rather unimaginative headline the next morning read 'Tottenham totter against Alf Ramsey's men'. But the copy was rather more enthusiastic, speaking of 'Gallant, incredible, little Ipswich Town' and the 'clean economic, accurate thrusts of Ipswich against the more subtle complicated football of the Spurs.' The report quoted Alf Ramsey as saying, 'It was a magnificent performance. We always looked like getting results and everyone played very well. It was the best victory in the history of the club.' Club captain Andy Nelson was reported as saying, 'They really excelled themselves, and it was a tremendous win. We were all fighting, and specially hard, to give our manager Alf Ramsey a proud return to White Hart Lane where he played so much of his football.' Indeed it must have been a particularly sweet victory for Alf Ramsey against his old club; a club which had been the first to win the double in over sixty years, just the season before.

The result inevitably kept Town in second place in the league table, but also meant they were now five points ahead of Tottenham Hotspur, surely making Town odds-on to finish as runners-up behind leaders, and continuing favourites for the title, Burnley. The other midweek fixtures produced these results:

14 March

Aston Villa	1–0	West Bromwich Albion
Cardiff City	1–1	Burnley
Sheffield United	1–1	Everton

Match No. 33
Saturday 17 March 1962
Venue: Portman Road
Ipswich Town 1–1 Blackpool   Attendance: 22,450

After the thrill of the top-of-the-table clash away at Tottenham Hotspur, it would be difficult for the next fixture to live up to anything like the same quality and excitement. So it proved with the visit of a Blackpool team who were heading for the obscurity of thirteenth place in the table. The Blackpool side showed just two changes from the one that had shared the points with Town up at Bloomfield Road back in October. In goal Bryan Harvey had replaced Tony Waiters, while in the forward line, despite being transfer-listed, Hauser, a South African, replaced Peterson. These then, were the full teams – Ipswich Town: Bailey; Carberry and Compton; Baxter, Nelson and Elsworthy; Stephenson, Moran, Crawford, Phillips and Leadbetter. Blackpool: Harvey; Armfield and Martin; Crawford B., Gratrix and Durie; Hill, Hauser, Charnley, Parry and Horne. The referee for this match was Mr G. McCabe of Sheffield.

After the magnificent win at White Hart Lane in the previous match, there was a degree of inevitability that this game would be a bit of an anti-climax. Unfortunately, as anti-climaxes go this was one of the more anti-climactic. The sports editor of the *East Anglian Daily Times* was moved to describe it as a 'shoddy' performance from Ipswich, characterised by erratic passing and defending.

Town only gave fleeting glimpses of skill and it was Ray Crawford who always looked the player most likely to produce something worthwhile. Indeed, it was Crawford who went on a run in the fourteenth minute the result of which was to create space for Doug Moran, who was able to take advantage and score from Crawford's subsequent pass.

Otherwise Town created few chances. Ted Phillips played well enough and tested Harvey in the Blackpool goal early in the second half; and though the ball rebounded out, Ray Crawford was unable to make it count. Phillips later fell awkwardly and was thought to have injured his wrist, while Jimmy Leadbetter picked up a knock to his knee that further hampered Town's attacking play.

In truth Blackpool had enough chances to have won the game and certainly deserved to get at least a point from it. For long periods they dominated possession and when they didn't have the ball they chased, tackled and kicked energetically to win it back. England inside forward Parry directed shots at the Town goal from all sorts of angles and missed every time. Horne was through with just Roy Bailey to beat, but missed, and Hauser failed to connect with a cross when the goal was gaping wide in front of him. In the Town defence Larry Carberry was the man of the match as he successfully marked left-winger Horne and made goal-line clearances from Hauser and Durie.

Then, with the game in its final minute and Town supporters urging the referee to blow his whistle for full time, England full-back Jimmy Armfield galloped upfield. He released Horne whose shot was blocked, but the ball fell to Ray Charnley who scored the equaliser, and his twenty-ninth goal of the season, with a scorching drive.

It had been a pretty mediocre game, much like the one earlier in the season at Bloomfield Road that had also ended in a 1–1 draw. This was the first time in twelve home league games that Town had not won, but fortunately they lost no ground as a result of this setback as Burnley had also drawn; 2–2 with Tottenham at Turf Moor. The result left the top of the table looking like this:

	P	W	D	L	F	A	Pts
Burnley	31	19	6	6	93	54	44
Ipswich Town	33	19	5	9	77	55	43
Everton	32	16	6	10	64	40	38
Tottenham Hotspur	32	15	8	10	65	57	38

Although Town now appeared to be pulling clear of Everton and, more importantly perhaps Tottenham Hotspur, they still trailed Burnley who had two matches in hand.

The other results from the weekend's fixtures were as follows:

Arsenal	1–1	Cardiff City
Birmingham City	0–2	Aston Villa
Bolton Wanderers	1–0	Manchester United
Burnley	2–2	Tottenham Hotspur
Everton	4–0	Chelsea
Fulham	5–2	Sheffield United
Leicester City	2–0	Blackburn Rovers
Manchester City	2–2	Wolverhampton Wanderers
Sheffield Wednesday	0–0	West Ham United
West Bromwich Albion	2–2	Nottingham Forest

One midweek fixture was played before the next round of Saturday fixtures:

Tuesday 20 March
Nottingham Forest   1–0   Manchester United

Match No. 34
Saturday 24 March 1962
Venue: The City Ground
Nottingham Forest 1–1 Ipswich Town   Attendance: 26,053

The disappointment of the Blackpool result was compounded by the news that Ted Phillips had in fact broken his thumb when he fell in that match. He was likely to miss this next game, the trip to the City Ground, Nottingham, and would be replaced by Dermot Curtis, whose only previous first team game this season had been as a replacement for Roy Stephenson in the 4–1 home win over Manchester United back in November. Curtis was currently the leading scorer in the Combination League, however, with twenty-one goals in twenty-six matches. Had Phillips played it would have been his 149th consecutive appearance for the Town.

Ray Crawford had played midweek having been selected for the English Football League XI against the Scottish League XI at Villa Park. The English won 4–3 and although Crawford hadn't scored, he came through the game with much credit for his performance.

For their part, Nottingham Forest came into the match having hit a decent patch of form. They had gleaned six points from their last four games to ease their worries of relegation, and now had a total of thirty points from thirty-four games. Town had a poor record at the City Ground having failed to score in each of their last three visits there; the most recent encounter being a 2–0 defeat in the 1954/55 season.

The teams lined up as follows – Nottingham Forest: Grummitt; Wilson and Gray; Winfield, McKinley and Iley; Rowland, Vowden, Julians, Quigley and Le Flem. Ipswich Town: Bailey; Carberry and Compton; Baxter, Nelson and Elsworthy; Stephenson, Moran, Crawford, Curtis and Leadbetter. The referee was Mr R.E. Smith of Newport.

With Nottingham Forest battling to pull away from the relegation zone and – on the evidence of the Blackpool game – Town losing their way a little, the prospects for this match did not look too bright. Regrettably this proved to be the case as, on a rock-hard pitch, Town turned in another poor display in a scrappy game in which neither team was much good in front of goal and both misplaced plenty of passes.

As in the Blackpool game the week before, it was Town who took a first-half lead. With eighteen minutes gone, Ray Crawford found himself wide on the right and he lofted a high cross toward the centre circle. Dermot Curtis met the cross and headed the ball forward for Doug Moran to run onto. Moran beat Iley and bore down on the goal; his shot hit the Forest keeper Grummitt, but Moran was able to strike home the rebound.

The lead lasted until the stroke of half time when Rowland rounded John Compton and sent in a low cross that Julian first controlled, before despatching the ball accurately past Roy Bailey.

Again, as in the Blackpool game, Town were fortunate at times not to concede other goals. More than once Roy Bailey came to their rescue after the defence had conspired to present chances to Nottingham Forest. Indeed, the headline in the *East Anglian Daily Times* report read 'Bailey earns Ipswich point at Nottingham'. The reporter was pessimistic after seeing this match and despite Town's eight-match unbeaten run, wrote of Town's Championship hopes fading. It was a poor display and only Dermot Curtis escaped criticism, although Jimmy Leadbetter had an excuse in that he was suffering from a stomach upset. Curtis in fact came close to snatching an undeserved winner for Town when, in the dying minutes, he beat Winfield in the air and sent a flying header goalwards. Other chances fell to Ray Crawford, who headed over, and to Doug Moran who, in the second half, mistakenly opted to lay the ball back when he was clean through on goal. For Nottingham Forest Quigley had the best chances, but he was as poor in front of goal as the Town players.

The draw left Nottingham Forest in sixteenth place in the table, three places better off than they would be after the full forty-two games. At the top end of the table, while Town had stumbled to take only a single point in Nottingham, Burnley had bagged both points with a 2–0 win over Aston Villa at Villa Park. The results meant Burnley had extended their lead over the Town to two points and they still had two games in hand as well.

Cardiff City had played on the Friday night and the day's other fixtures produced the following results:

23 March
| Cardiff City | 0–3 | Fulham |

24 March
Aston Villa	0–2	Burnley
Blackburn Rovers	1–1	West Bromwich Albion
Blackpool	1–0	Birmingham City
Chelsea	2–3	Arsenal
Manchester United	1–1	Sheffield Wednesday
Sheffield United	3–1	Bolton Wanderers
Tottenham Hotspur	3–1	Everton
West Ham United	0–4	Manchester City
Wolverhampton Wanderers	1–1	Leicester City

Match No. 35
Wednesday 28 March 1962
Venue: Filbert Street
Leicester City 0–2 Ipswich Town   Attendance: 19,068

This was a rearranged match that had originally been scheduled for Saturday 30 December. The original game was one of thirty-three postponements that Saturday which was a new record, with just twelve English league matches being played.

After poor performances in their last two games and with Ted Phillips still out with a broken thumb, it was, on the face of it, possibly not the best time for Town to have to play a second game in five days. To compound matters there was still no news on the morning of the match as to whether the Army would release Bill Baxter to play. He was to play against the Belgian Army on the following Saturday and so would miss the fixture at home to Wolves, and the fear was that they would not grant him leave ahead of that game; they didn't. It would be the first time in any competitive fixture this season that Baxter was missing from the Town team. Baxter's replacement was Reg Pickett, the only player in the Town squad who already had a Championship medal to his name, which he had won with Portsmouth back in 1950. It was to be Reg Pickett's 150th appearance for Town.

Leicester were heading for a modest finish of fourteenth in the league table, but had a settled side that showed only one change from the side that had lost 1–0 at Portman Road the previous Boxing Day; the change being the inclusion of Michael Stringfellow in place of John Mitten. Leicester manager Matt Gillies might have also included David Gibson in his team, but like Bill Baxter, Gibson was in the Army and he had picked up an injury playing for them at Woolwich on the previous Saturday. The full teams were – Leicester City: Banks; Chalmers and Norman; McLintock, King and Appleton; Riley, Cheesebrough, Walsh, Keyworth and Stringfellow. Ipswich Town: Bailey; Carberry and Compton; Pickett, Nelson and Elsworthy; Stephenson, Moran, Crawford, Curtis and Leadbetter. The referee for this match was Mr K.A. Collinge of Altrincham.

This was a fast, thrilling match played on a muddy pitch. Ipswich were very much on top of their game, always looking confident and full of running. Early on, Stephenson headed wide from a Leadbetter corner, but after only eight minutes Town took the lead when Moran centred the ball and Crawford ran on to it at full speed to send a flashing header past a rather bemused Gordon Banks in the Leicester goal.

But Leicester fought back from this early setback and on nineteen minutes just Elsworthy and Bailey stood between the fabulously named Albert Cheesebrough and the goal, but fortunately for Town, Elsworthy was able to force him into shooting wide. Further chances ensued at both ends with Bailey saving well from Jim Walsh, and Banks denying both Crawford and Moran.

After thirty-five minutes Ken Keyworth had a glorious chance to level the scores. Roy Bailey could only punch a Cheesebrough centre; Keyworth collected the rebound from Bailey's fist, but with time to control his shot, he sent the ball over the crossbar. Then Bailey again preserved Town's lead, keeping out a drive from Michael Stringfellow.

The game carried on being very much an end-to-end affair. But with forty-eight minutes gone Town were able to get a firmer grip on the game and double their lead when, from a goalmouth scramble, the ball came to Roy Stephenson who shot through a crowd of players into the net.

Leicester would not lie down, however, and thereafter probably had more chances than Town, with Bailey being the busier of the two goalkeepers. But Ipswich played well on the break, with Leadbetter hitting several probing, defence-splitting passes from deep positions and Ray Crawford was also on top form. Reg Pickett had settled into the team very quickly and Elsworthy's and Nelson's height was sufficient to cut out most Leicester attacks, which mainly came at the instigation of Walsh. Town held firm and with there being no further goals the two points went to Ipswich.

Match No. 36
Saturday 31 March 1962
Venue: Portman Road
Ipswich Town 3–2 Wolverhampton Wanderers   Attendance: 23,153

The good news prior to the Wolves game was that Ted Phillips had had the plaster removed from his broken thumb and would be fit to play. There was, however, a doubt over John Compton who had received a knock to his thigh; Ken Malcolm was on standby to take his place, but in the end he was not required. Billy Baxter, however, had to play for the Army and so Reg Pickett continued in his place in the number four shirt. The Wolves team showed four changes to the one that had beaten Town at Molineux back in November; the new faces being Finlayson, Kirkham, McParland and Crowe. Both McParland and Crowe had already faced Town this season but for different clubs; Aston Villa and Blackburn Rovers. These were the full teams – Ipswich Town: Bailey; Carberry and Compton; Pickett, Nelson and Elsworthy; Stephenson, Moran, Crawford, Phillips and Leadbetter. Wolverhampton Wanderers: Finlayson; Stuart and Showell; Kirkham, Slater and Flowers; Crowe, Murray, McParland, Broadbent and Wharton. The referee was Mr S. Yates of Bristol.

As had happened in their previous four games, it was Town who scored first in this match. But they had to wait until the twentieth minute before they took the lead and in truth it was courtesy of the Wolves' defence as Slater hauled down Ray Crawford and Mr Yates awarded a penalty. As usual, up stepped Ted Phillips and he smashed the ball into the roof of the net. The lead was to last for only four minutes, however, as a Wolves corner from the right-hand side fell to Flowers some twenty-five yards from goal and he volleyed the ball into the goal off the inside of a post.

But Town regained the lead later in the first half, this time through Ray Crawford. The goal came indirectly as a result of Wolves players disputing one of Mr Yates' decisions. After McParland had argued with a linesman, Mr Yates spoke to Stuart and then started play again with a drop ball. Town gained possession from this and Doug Moran fed the ball out to Roy Stephenson who then sent a ball into the middle of the field for Ray Crawford to chase. Crawford got to the ball, controlled it, and beat Finlayson to restore Town's lead. The lead did not last until half time, however, as, with the Town defence in disarray, Peter McParland beat Roy Bailey for Wolverhampton's second equaliser of the afternoon.

Having come back from behind for a second time it now looked as though Wolverhampton Wanderers would go on to win the match as Town struggled to find their form. In the second half Wolves attacked Town again and again, applying relentless pressure. Wharton must have hit half a dozen shots over the crossbar for Wolves, and England international Ron Flowers was having an exceptional game. Town meanwhile may have been handicapped by an injury to Ray Crawford early on and of course Ted Phillips was only just back after his two-game absence. But whatever the reason, this was not a good Town performance.

The game was drawing to a close and despite their many chances Wolves had not managed to score again to take the lead. There were just two minutes to go as Ted Phillips crossed from the right. The ball reached a completely unmarked Ray Crawford; his shot ran across the face of the goal but Doug Moran managed to slide in, reach the ball and guide it into the net to score the winner for Town. Victory belonged to Ipswich because they had taken their chances and Wolverhampton had not.

Town had been very lucky to win this match, but that was forgotten as for the first time, as the *East Anglian* sports headline read, 'Town top the Championship table at last'. The top of the table looked like this:

	P	W	D	L	F	A	Pts
Ipswich Town	36	21	6	9	83	58	48
Burnley	32	20	6	6	95	54	46
Tottenham Hotspur	34	16	8	10	68	58	40

Because of the FA Cup semi-finals (Burnley v Fulham and Tottenham v Manchester United), there was not a full programme of Division One fixtures this weekend and two matches had been played on the previous Friday evening; these were the results from all the league games.

30 March 1962

Birmingham City	2–1	Blackburn Rovers
Everton	2–2	Blackpool

31 March 1962

Arsenal	4–5	Aston Villa
Bolton Wanderers	4–2	Chelsea
Ipswich Town	3–2	Wolverhampton Wanderers
Manchester City	1–1	Sheffield United
West Bromwich Albion	0–1	West Ham United

So the eighth and penultimate month of the season came to a close. It had been a crucial month to Town as they had played seven games and taken fourteen points despite not always playing particularly well. Their biggest rivals, Burnley and Tottenham, had by comparison only managed to harvest six points and three points respectively from four games. Not only had Town accumulated a good stock of points, but they were stealing a march on their rivals by actually playing league games rather than acquiring a backlog of fixtures.

   The complete Division One table with just one month remaining therefore lined up like this:

	P	W	D	L	F	A	Pts	Goal Ave.
Ipswich Town	36	21	6	9	83	58	48	1.43
Burnley	32	20	6	6	95	54	46	1.76
Tottenham Hotspur	34	16	8	10	68	58	40	1.17
Everton	34	16	7	11	67	45	39	1.49
Sheffield United	34	16	7	11	46	55	39	0.84
West Ham United	35	15	8	12	63	67	38	0.94
Aston Villa	35	15	7	13	47	45	37	1.04
Blackpool	35	13	10	12	59	56	36	1.05
Sheffield Wednesday	33	14	6	13	55	44	34	1.25
Blackburn Rovers	33	12	10	11	41	41	34	1.00
Manchester City	35	14	6	15	68	70	34	0.97
Arsenal	33	12	9	12	53	53	33	1.00
West Bromwich Albion	36	10	12	14	65	63	32	1.03
Manchester United	33	12	8	13	55	58	32	0.95
Wolverhampton Wanderers	36	12	8	16	62	71	32	0.87
Birmingham City	35	12	8	15	51	68	32	0.75
Leicester City	34	13	5	16	54	54	31	1.00
Nottingham Forest	35	11	9	15	55	64	31	0.86
Bolton Wanderers	34	12	7	15	49	58	31	0.84
Cardiff City	34	7	13	14	38	58	27	0.66
Fulham	33	9	6	18	49	60	24	0.82
Chelsea	35	9	6	20	54	78	24	0.69

Meanwhile . . .

In the world beyond Ipswich one of the most interesting stories of the month was the demise of Accrington Stanley Football Club. On 6 March they tendered their resignation from the Football League, as they buckled under the weight of £60,000-worth of debts. It seems there was no temporary administration for them. Two days later their misfortune was brought into sharp relief as West Ham United paid a then record transfer fee for a British club when they paid Crystal Palace £65,000 (actually £60,000 plus Ron Brett) for the signature of Johnny Byrne. Much as now, the inequalities within professional football were gross, the fee for a single player being equal to the sum necessary to save an entire club. The previous record fee had been £55,000 paid by Manchester City to Huddersfield Town for Denis Law.

Away from football there were a couple of health-related stories in the news during March 1962. In Wales 87,000 people were vaccinated in order to prevent a smallpox epidemic, and in London the Royal College of Physicians urged the government to increase purchase tax on cigarettes in an attempt to reduce the number of cases of lung cancer.

Abroad, the French were in the final throes of hanging onto a part of their 'empire' as their troops fought with Algerian rebels. March saw the machine-gunning of fifty Algerians by French soldiers but also a ceasefire. At the other end of the Mediterranean, Syrian and Israeli forces clashed by the Sea of Galilee.

Returning to lighter matters back home in Ipswich, there was a comedy double bill on at the Gaumont cinema with Norman Wisdom starring in *The Bulldog Breed* and Kenneth More and Shirley-Ann Field appearing in *The Man in the Moon*. Also at the Gaumont, but live on stage, was Billy Fury. At the town's other two cinemas the films showing contrasted quite strongly with one another, with dark goings on in the *The Pit and the Pendulum* at the Odeon, while there was nothing darker than Cliff Richard's sun tan in *The Young Ones* at the ABC.

On stage at the Ipswich Theatre in Tower Street (now the Old Rep pub) you could see *A Man for All Seasons*, the story of Sir Thomas More, statesman to Henry VIII and contemporary of Ipswich's very own Sir Thomas Wolsey.

On 22 March Elvis Presley was knocked off the top of the music charts, where he had been for the past month. The new number one was 'Wonderful Land' by the Shadows and it was destined to stay at the top until beyond the end of the football season. How appropriate it was that a song with such a title should be the soundtrack for the months when Ipswich Town led the table and would then win the League Championship.

In the news locally there was talk of Ipswich Corporation (nowadays known as the Borough Council) extending the borough to take in Rushmere. This drew a rather severe response from Brigadier P.L. Lindsay, an East Suffolk County Councillor, who was quoted as having said, 'This was very like Hitlerism or Communism, once they got a foot in they wanted to take the whole thing over.'

Finally, the Town's success was being noticed by at least one local business as Botwood's garage gave their advertising a football theme. Advertising the Austin Seven, Botwood's advert read, 'Another Home Win. League champions for years and years Austin have earned maximum points again.' Was this a premonition on the part of Botwood's?

April

Match No. 37
Saturday 7 April 1962
Venue: Old Trafford
Manchester United 5–0 Ipswich Town   Attendance: 24,976

Flushed with the success of having made history by being the first Town team to be top of the Football League, Alf Ramsey's side rolled on to their next game, away to Manchester United. It was Town's first ever visit in the league to Old Trafford but they had of course played there in the FA Cup in 1958, only days before the Munich air crash. Roy Bailey, John Elsworthy and Jimmy Leadbetter had all played in that game in 1958.

Back in the early 1960s Manchester United were more or less just another club from a provincial English city. The phenomenon of crowds of 50,000 or 60,000 people at Old Trafford for every match was not known in 1962. The M5 and M6 motorways were yet to be completed so the Surrey, Devon, Norfolk and Essex branches of the Manchester United Supporters Club, if they even existed, had to stay at home and listen to the radio or, heaven forbid, support their local teams. Moreover, Manchester United were nothing special as a team; they were destined to finish fifteenth in the league in 1962, beneath all these Lancashire rivals: Burnley, Bolton Wanderers, Manchester City and Blackpool. Blackburn Rovers were the only Lancastrians to finish below United. It was no great surprise therefore that for this match a crowd of less than 25,000 turned up.

For Town, Ray Crawford had played for England against Austria during the preceding week. Unfortunately he had received a kick on his foot in the early stages of that match and was now not fit enough to face Manchester United. Dermot Curtis was due to join the Eire squad for their match the day after the Manchester United game, but he was nevertheless drafted into the Town side as Crawford's replacement. Bill Baxter was now available for selection, however, and he replaced Reg Pickett in the side.

Manchester United had to pick themselves up from being defeated FA Cup semi-finalists against Tottenham Hotspur the previous weekend. It wasn't to be a problem for too many of that losing team, however, as Matt

Busby made eight changes to his team. These then were the two sides at Old Trafford that day – Manchester United: Briggs; Brennan and Dunne; Stiles, Foulkes and Setters; Moir, Giles, Quixall, McMillan and Charlton. Ipswich Town: Bailey; Carberry and Compton; Baxter, Nelson and Elsworthy; Stephenson, Moran, Curtis, Phillips and Leadbetter. The referee was Mr R.J. Simons of Carlisle.

There is little to say from a Town perspective about this match – quite simply, they were outplayed. After the first ten minutes there was not a single Town attack of any worth. Only Roy Bailey emerged from the game with any sort of credit. The *East Anglian Daily Times* report declined to give much detail, as there was not much to say about Town in a one-sided game. Roy Stephenson received virtually nothing of the ball in his right wing position. Both Ted Phillips and Jimmy Leadbetter were said to have been poor. Doug Moran toiled away up front but to little effect. For their part Manchester United ripped Town's defence to pieces and their players were always quicker to the ball and always intent on taking the game to Ipswich. Relative league positions counted for nothing.

The score was 2–0 at half time with Albert Quixall scoring in the fourteenth and twentieth minutes. He completed his hat-trick five minutes into the second half and then the rout was confirmed late on with goals from Nobby Stiles and Maurice Setters in the eighty-fourth and eighty-fifth minutes respectively.

It was the heaviest defeat of the season for Town and the first league defeat since 21 January. But still they had got off lightly, with both Bobby Charlton and Sammy McMillan coming close to making it 7–0 by having had shots that struck the woodwork. To add to a miserable afternoon the home crowd constantly barracked Town captain Andy Nelson after he committed a foul on Quixall. Andy Nelson was quoted in the *East Anglian* as having said, 'This must be the biggest hammering that we have ever received.'

Initially the result did not mean that Town were knocked off their perch at the top of the table for although Burnley did not lose heavily like Town, they did not win; having to be content with a single point from a draw at Wolverhampton.

West Ham and Birmingham had played on the previous Friday night and here is that result and the others from Saturday 7 April plus those from the following week's midweek fixtures:

6 April
| West Ham United | 2–2 | Birmingham City |

7 April
Aston Villa	3–0	Bolton Wanderers
Blackburn Rovers	1–1	Everton
Blackpool	2–1	Fulham
Cardiff City	0–4	Leicester City

Chelsea	1–1	Manchester City
Nottingham Forest	0–1	Arsenal
Sheffield United	1–1	West Bromwich Albion
Tottenham Hotspur	4–0	Sheffield Wednesday
Wolverhampton Wanderers	1–1	Burnley

9 April

| Tottenham Hotspur | 2–4 | Sheffield United |

10 April

| Blackburn Rovers | 3–0 | Manchester United |

11 April

Bolton Wanderers	0–0	Burnley
Fulham	5–2	Arsenal
Leicester City	2–0	Chelsea
Manchester City	1–4	Birmingham City

The midweek results did knock Town off the top of the table but still Burnley had only drawn. With the league championship campaign having now entered its final month, the top of the table looked like this:

	P	W	D	L	F	A	Pts
Burnley	34	20	8	6	96	55	48
Ipswich Town	37	21	6	10	83	63	48
Tottenham Hotspur	35	17	8	10	72	58	42
Sheffield United	36	17	8	11	53	58	42

Significantly for Ipswich, Tottenham were well beaten at home by Sheffield United on the Monday night, which meant that Spurs could only equal Town's points total if they won their other two games in hand. In the light of Town's thrashing at Old Trafford it did look, however, as though Burnley were still the odds-on favourites to lift the title, despite having failed to win either of their last two games.

Match No. 38
Saturday 14 April 1962
Venue : Portman Road
Ipswich Town 1–0 Cardiff City   Attendance: 17,693

With only five games left to play and Town in second place in the table, this next match at home to Cardiff City oddly drew the second smallest crowd of the season at Portman Road. Perhaps people felt that Town's chances of taking the Championship had evaporated in the 5–0 defeat at Old Trafford; perhaps supporters were too downhearted, or perhaps the visit of the club second to bottom of the First Division was simply an unattractive proposition on a spring afternoon.

Cardiff City were struggling and would continue to do so right up to the very end of the season when they were destined to be relegated to Division Two. The Bluebirds had lost their previous game, a home fixture against Leicester City, by four goals to nil and they were just one point ahead of bottom club Fulham. Their full record for the season so far read like this:

	P	W	D	L	F	A	Pts
Cardiff City	36	7	13	16	38	64	26

No doubt searching for some sort of inspiration that would transform his team, the Cardiff manager made six changes to the team that had lost to Leicester.

For Town, Ray Crawford was fit again and he returned to the side in place of Dermot Curtis. John Elsworthy had strained a stomach muscle, however, and he was not fit enough to play. Reg Pickett now made a quick return to the side having deputised for Billy Baxter a couple of games earlier, as he took up John Elsworthy's number six shirt. The teams were – Ipswich Town: Bailey; Carberry and Compton; Baxter, Nelson and Pickett; Stephenson, Moran, Crawford, Phillips and Leadbetter. Cardiff City: John; Sitfall and Milne; Baker, Rankmore and Hole; McCarthy, King, Charles, Durban and Pickrell. The referee was Mr J.R. Loynton of Solihull.

As had been the pattern in all but one of the past five matches since the win at White Hart Lane, Town did not play particularly well. Despite the two clubs being at opposite ends of the league table it was a close match. The conditions were difficult, but that was the same for both teams and though Town had more of the possession than Cardiff City, they failed to impress. Cardiff City meanwhile were enthusiastic, but that was about all.

Chances fell to both sides in the first half with Barry Hole hitting the crossbar for the visitors and Welsh international Mel Charles also missing two opportunities, although Andy Nelson generally kept him quiet. After twenty-four minutes Roy Stephenson crossed from the right-hand side; Cardiff's goalkeeper Dilwyn John misjudged the flight of the ball and Crawford got to it first to head goalwards. The ball may have gone into the net unassisted but just to make sure, Doug Moran nipped in to send it over the line.

Thereafter it was an even game. Jimmy Leadbetter and Doug Moran missed chances but often Town's attacks were too predictable. Roy Stephenson beat the full-back a number of times but his crosses were not dangerous enough. Ray Crawford had a quiet game after his return from injury and in defence stand-in half-back Reg Pickett played very well. Roy Bailey did his bit for the win too when, with just four minutes remaining, he stretched to save well after Peter King sent in a shot from only eight yards.

The match had not been a classic by any means, but at this stage of the season it was the result that was all-important. What is more, the *East Anglian* was able to lead its sports page with the headline 'Ipswich Town regain league leadership'. While Town had won, rivals Burnley had taken on Town's tormentors from the week before, Manchester United. Just to show that they had nothing personal against Ipswich, United proceeded to beat Burnley too, by three goals to one. The top of the table now looked like this:

	P	W	D	L	F	A	Pts
Ipswich Town	38	23	6	10	84	63	50
Burnley	36	20	9	7	97	58	49

Everton were in third place, some seven points behind Town on forty-three points. The possibility of lifting the Championship now seemed to be on again as Burnley were systematically failing to win their games in hand. Even the generally taciturn Alf Ramsey admitted they had a chance and was quoted in the *East Anglian* as saying 'Our chance must be awfully good, but it is up to ourselves to win our remaining matches.' The day's other fixtures produced these results:

Arsenal	3–1	Wolverhampton Wanderers
Birmingham City	3–0	Sheffield United
Bolton Wanderers	6–1	Nottingham Forest
Burnley	1–3	Manchester United
Everton	3–0	West Ham United
Fulham	2–0	Blackburn Rovers
Man City	1–0	Aston Villa
Sheffield Wednesday	3–2	Blackpool
West Bromwich Albion	4–0	Chelsea

Ipswich were up to date with their fixtures, but a handful of clubs had games to catch up on owing to postponements earlier in the season. The following midweek therefore saw a handful of these rearranged fixtures. One result in particular was of significance to Ipswich. Burnley played one of their two games in hand, meeting Blackburn Rovers at Turf Moor in a local East Lancashire derby, and most unexpectedly it was Blackburn who took the points with single-goal victory.

16 April
Manchester United	2–3	Arsenal

17 April
Burnley	0–1	Blackburn Rovers
Fulham	1–1	Tottenham Hotspur

Match No. 39
Friday 20 April 1962
Venue: Portman Road
Ipswich Town 2–2 Arsenal   Attendance: 30,649

For this crucial game the Portman Road ground welcomed its first ever 30,000-plus crowd, exceeding the previous record (set against Norwich City in the FA Cup three months earlier) by almost 1,000. Even then, hundreds of supporters were locked out of the ground. This was the first ever fixture between Arsenal and Town as they had never previously been in the same division of the Football League. Arsenal had, of course, been in Division One continuously since 1919 and dominated the league championship back in the 1930s, but their last Championship success had been in 1953. Since then they had only finished in the top five on three occasions and had been very much a mid-table side in the other years.

John Elsworthy was fit to face Arsenal and came back into the team in place of Reg Pickett. For Arsenal, Eddie Clamp, twice a Championship-winner with Wolves, was suspended after being cautioned in a game at Old Trafford the previous week and so missed the game. These were the full teams – Ipswich Town: Bailey; Carberry and Compton; Baxter, Nelson and Elsworthy; Stephenson, Moran, Crawford, Phillips and Leadbetter. Arsenal: Kelsey; Magill and McCullough; Brown, Neill and Petts; McLeod, Griffiths, Strong, Eastham and Skirton. The referee, with an appreciation of alliteration, was Mr G.W. Grundy of Grimsby.

The action in this match all came in the second half; the first half being little more than an hors d'oeuvre. Town began the game looking tense and pent-up while Arsenal by contrast were relaxed and calm. Town did have attacks but often they retreated and played a negative game, fearful perhaps of giving anything away. For Arsenal, George Eastham was excellent; he dominated much of the play and might have won the game for Arsenal late on. The real drama began, however, ten minutes after the restart when Arsenal won a corner that was taken short before the ball was fed to George Eastham who crossed. Alan Skirton headed the ball down and Scottish international John McLeod drove it beyond Roy Bailey to give Arsenal the lead.

Just four minutes later George Eastham beat three Town players in the middle of the park before moving across to the right. Then, with his back to goal he hooked the ball over his head and into the goal off the far post to double Arsenal's lead. It was an amazing goal that even some Ipswich fans felt moved to applaud.

Things looked black for Town but five minutes later Terry Neill offered hope to them as he brought down Ray Crawford in the penalty area. Naturally, Ted Phillips scored from the resultant spot-kick. The relief was tangible and the home crowd surged onto the pitch, as the cramped Portman Road stands simply could not contain the elation.

Town still needed to score again to get even a point from the game, but the penalty proved to be a watershed and from now on they dominated proceedings. Phillips forced Kelsey into a fine save and also hit the crossbar, while Billy Baxter had a header that the Town players felt had crossed the goal line.

The game was nearing its end and still Town were searching for that second goal. With five minutes left, Roy Stephenson's corner kick was knocked back to Ted Phillips; he shot, but his effort was blocked and fell to Jimmy Leadbetter who seemed to squeeze himself through to force the ball over the line and score. Once again the crowd sprang from the stands and onto the pitch.

Town had had to come back from two goals behind to claim the draw, so it could be seen to be a point won rather than a point lost. But Burnley still had a game in hand and they had won their game at home to Blackpool, so they now had the same number of points as Town and returned to the top of the table by virtue of their superior goal average. The top of the table now looked like this:

	P	W	D	L	F	A	Pts
Burnley	38	21	9	8	99	59	51
Ipswich Town	39	22	7	10	86	63	51
Tottenham Hotspur	38	18	10	10	80	63	46
Everton	38	18	9	11	76	48	45
Sheffield United	38	17	9	12	56	64	43

These were the other results that day:

Burnley	2–0	Blackpool
Chelsea	4–5	Wolverhampton Wanderers
Everton	4–1	Birmingham City
Manchester City	3–1	Sheffield Wednesday
Tottenham Hotspur	4–1	Blackburn Rovers
West Ham United	4–1	Cardiff City

Match No. 40
Saturday 21 April 1962
Venue: Stamford Bridge
Chelsea 2–2 Ipswich Town   Attendance: 28,462

The draw with Arsenal the day before could be viewed as a point lost, particularly as it was only the second time in fifteen home league games that Town had not won. But in view of how Town had played overall and the fact that they had had to recover from a 2–0 deficit, the truth was probably that it was a point gained. The result nevertheless meant that it was even more important to get something from this next game, preferably a victory.

Despite some less than convincing performances of late, the formbook still favoured an Ipswich win. Chelsea were bottom of the league and if they failed to win this match they would be relegated. The two teams lined up like this – Chelsea: McNally; Shellito and Butler; Malcolm, Mortimore and Upton; Brabrook, Murray, Bridges, Blunstone and Harrison. Ipswich Town: Bailey; Carberry and Compton; Baxter, Nelson and Elsworthy; Stephenson, Moran, Crawford, Phillips and Leadbetter. The referee was Mr Les Hamer of Bolton.

Chelsea were competing for their First Division survival and from the play it appeared very much as if this inspired them more than the hopes of a league championship win motivated the Town. In the first half an hour Chelsea had the chances to be 5–0 up, but in reality they scored just once. After twenty-five minutes Chelsea right-winger Peter Brabrook beat three defenders and fired a rocket of a shot into the net from a tight angle to give the home side the lead. Town had got off lightly so far, but Chelsea were to score the second goal that all their early pressure warranted, and ten minutes later Brabrook was involved again as he swung over a deep cross to Blunstone who tapped the ball back into the middle for Barry Bridges to score.

From the way Town were playing it looked more like they were the team staring relegation in the face and Chelsea were the ones chasing honours. Town had been completely outplayed in the first half and were deservedly two goals behind.

Alf Ramsey could not have been at all pleased with his players and their improved showing in the second half indicated that he had sorted a few things out during the interval. With an hour gone Ray Crawford spread a pass out to Jimmy Leadbetter on the flank. Crawford then ran on towards goal and called for the return ball from Leadbetter who duly sent over a lob that Crawford met with a header past the helpless McNally in the Chelsea goal.

Town were back in the match and now had the upper hand. They were denied a penalty claim when McNally grabbed Crawford around the waist but Mr Hamer the referee gave a corner instead. The corner kick however, was met by Chelsea half-back John Mortimore, who proceeded to punch the ball away from the goal. This time the referee spotted the infringement and awarded a penalty, which Ted Phillips duly scored to level the game.

Although Chelsea tried to retaliate, and indeed missed a couple of good chances before the end, there was to be no further scoring and Town had claimed another point. The result relegated Chelsea to Division Two for the first time in thirty-two years. Just seven years beforehand, Chelsea had won the Championship themselves.

A draw had not been enough for Chelsea today, but the question for Town was whether a single point was enough for them to maintain the pressure on Burnley who were still the favourites to lift the title. The fates were in Town's favour, however, as Burnley lost away at Sheffield United and so Town returned to the top of the table once again.

	P	W	D	L	F	A	Pts
Ipswich Town	40	22	8	10	87	66	52
Burnley	39	21	9	9	99	61	51

The day's other results were as follows:

Aston Villa	8–3	Leicester City*
Blackburn Rovers	2–3	Bolton Wanderers
Blackpool	3–1	Manchester City
Cardiff City	3–2	Birmingham City
Manchester United	1–1	Everton
Nottingham Forest	3–1	Sheffield Wednesday
Sheffield United	2–0	Burnley
Tottenham Hotspur	1–2	West Bromwich Albion
West Ham United	2–4	Arsenal
Wolverhampton Wanderers	1–3	Fulham

* Yes, Aston Villa really did beat Leicester City 8–3.

Match No. 41
Monday 23 April 1962
Venue: Highbury
Arsenal 0–3 Ipswich Town   Attendance: 44,964

The return game against Arsenal at Highbury came just three days after their first meeting at Portman Road. Although Good Friday's game had been the first competitive meeting between the two clubs, Town had in fact played a competitive match at Highbury before. Oddly, that game had been just three months before in the third round of the FA Cup, when Town's tie with Luton Town went to a second replay and Highbury was chosen as the neutral venue for the match. If there were any omens to be had from that they were good ones, as Town had beaten Luton by five goals to one.

    The Arsenal team showed two changes from the one that had drawn at Portman Road. At right-half Eddie Clamp returned from suspension to replace Laurie Brown, while in the forward line Daniel Clapton took the place of Alan Skirton. Town showed no changes from the side that had claimed a point at Stamford Bridge two days before and had played Arsenal the day before that. The match drew the biggest gate of the day in England, and included a 5,000-strong travelling contingent from Ipswich. Arsenal: Kelsey; Magill and McCullough; Clamp, Neill and Petts; Clapton, Griffiths, Strong, Eastham and McLeod. Ipswich Town: Bailey; Carberry and Compton; Baxter, Nelson and Elsworthy; Stephenson, Moran, Crawford, Phillips and Leadbetter. The referee was Mr A. Holland of Barnsley.

The contest started off evenly but with Arsenal, as you might expect of the home side, pressing more for the opening goal. Bailey had to tip a shot from John McLeod over the crossbar and Arfon Griffiths and Geoff Strong also tried their luck with shots on the Town goal. On fourteen minutes, however, Larry Carberry, pushing up from full-back, won a corner. Roy Stephenson whipped over a high cross from which Ted Phillips sent a looping header beyond keeper Jack Kelsey and under the crossbar to give Town the lead. The travelling fans from Ipswich were ecstatic and roared their team on. Roy Stephenson then sent in a low cross to the far post where Phillips dummied, allowing the ball to run to Ray Crawford who scored from a narrow angle, giving Town a two-goal lead.

Arsenal probably had more of the play in the first half – they had a chance to score when Clapton beat Compton and Elsworthy to set up Griffiths who hit his shot straight at Bailey – but Town still created chances of their own. After twenty-one minutes Terry Neill handled the ball to prevent Ray Crawford cutting inside him into the penalty area. Ted Phillips took the resultant free-kick, but Kelsey saved it. After half an hour, Jimmy Leadbetter's incisive pass released Doug Moran who ran between two Arsenal defenders and beat Kelsey with his shot, only for Northern Ireland international McCullough to clear the ball off the goal line. At the other end Arsenal appealed in vain for a penalty, accusing Billy Baxter of having handled the ball, and on forty minutes George Eastham chipped the ball over Roy Bailey into the net, but Strong and Griffiths were pulled up for offside and the goal was disallowed.

In the second half Arsenal were nowhere near as threatening as they had been. Perhaps most crucially, Billy Baxter succeeded in keeping a tight rein on Arsenal's exceptional forward George Eastham. On the other hand Town continued to create good chances. Both Moran and Crawford had shots that missed. Then, Ray Crawford collected the ball from a throw-in. He took the ball past both Petts and McCullough and nutmegged Terry Neill before shooting the ball past Jack Kelsey and sending Town into a three-goal lead before a delirious band of supporters. It was surely Ray Crawford's best goal of the season.

Close to the end Town almost claimed a fourth goal as Ted Phillips' volley was saved by Kelsey diving at full stretch, and then Kelsey saved again from Billy Baxter.

The result was just what Town needed to keep what pressure they could on Burnley. A defeat would have meant that the Championship was Burnley's, but Town had played well and won well to keep their hopes alive. The result was in fact seldom in doubt, and the *East Anglian Daily Times* quoted Alf Ramsey as having said it had been 'a top rate display.' Despite the win, and the fact that Burnley had only drawn again (1–1 away at Blackpool), the odds still seemed to be in Burnley's favour because they had a superior goal average and they were still favourites to win their remaining fixtures at home to already-relegated Chelsea and away to Sheffield Wednesday. Town also still had to beat Aston Villa. This was summed up in the lengthy sports headline in the *East Anglian*, which read 'Ipswich town trounce Arsenal – but title race still in the balance'. One positive was that Town were now guaranteed to be runners-up at least, whatever happened over the next ten days. The top of the Championship table now looked like this:

	P	W	D	L	F	A	Pts
Ipswich Town	41	23	8	10	91	67	54
Burnley	40	21	10	9	100	62	52
Tottenham Hotspur	40	19	10	11	82	65	48

These were the results from the remainder of the matches in the division:

Aston Villa	5–1	Nottingham Forest
Blackburn Rovers	0–1	Tottenham Hotspur
Blackpool	1–1	Burnley
Bolton Wanderers	1–0	Leicester City
Cardiff City	3–0	West Ham United
Fulham	1–2	West Bromwich Albion
Manchester United	0–1	Sheffield United
Sheffield Wednesday	1–0	Manchester City
Wolverhampton Wanderers	1–1	Chelsea

Town had now completed all but one of their league fixtures, but there were other clubs that had suffered more postponements owing to bad weather and greater involvement in the cup competitions, and so before the final Saturday there were a number of midweek fixtures to be played; these were the results from them:

24 April

Birmingham City	0–0	Everton
Leicester City	1–1	Bolton Wanderers
Nottingham Forest	2–0	Aston Villa
Sheffield United	2–3	Manchester United
West Bromwich Albion	2–0	Fulham

26 April

Blackburn Rovers	0–2	Sheffield Wednesday

With these games played the First Division table now looked like this on the eve of the final Saturday of the Football League season:

	P	W	D	L	F	A	Pts	Goal Ave.
Ipswich Town	41	23	8	10	91	67	54	1.36
Burnley	40	21	10	9	100	62	52	1.61
Tottenham Hotspur	40	19	10	11	82	65	48	1.26
Everton	40	18	11	11	77	49	47	1.57
Sheffield United	41	19	9	13	61	67	47	0.91
Aston Villa	40	18	7	15	63	52	43	1.21
Sheffield Wednesday	40	18	6	16	65	56	42	1.16
West Ham United	40	16	10	14	72	79	42	0.91
West Bromwich Albion	41	14	13	14	76	66	41	1.15
Arsenal	40	15	11	14	67	69	41	0.97
Blackpool	41	15	11	15	69	88	41	0.78
Bolton Wanderers	41	15	10	16	61	66	40	0.92
Manchester United	41	15	9	17	72	73	39	0.99
Manchester City	41	16	7	18	75	80	39	0.94
Blackburn Rovers	41	14	11	16	49	54	39	0.91
Leicester City	40	16	6	18	68	67	38	1.01
Birmingham City	41	14	10	17	63	78	38	0.81
Wolverhampton Wanderers	41	13	10	18	71	83	36	0.86
Nottingham Forest	41	13	10	18	62	77	36	0.81
Fulham	40	12	7	21	62	70	31	0.89
Cardiff City	40	9	13	18	45	71	31	0.63
Chelsea R	**41**	**9**	**9**	**23**	**62**	**93**	**27**	**0.67**

There was now just one match left for Ipswich Town in their first ever season in the First Division of the Football League and they had a chance of making English football history.

Meanwhile . . .
It was budget month in Britain as on 9 April the chancellor announced cuts in purchase tax, the forerunner of VAT. The top rate payable on what were then classified as luxury items such as cars, television sets and radios, fell from 55 per cent to 45 per cent, which makes our present 20 per cent VAT look pretty paltry. At those rates it certainly wasn't a stealth tax. The rate was cut to 15 per cent on sweets, soft drinks and ice cream and the budget was dubbed 'the ice cream budget'. The cheaper sweets were a good thing providing cheaper comfort food for those people struggling through the grip of a potato shortage that meant the traditional British diet of chips was, if only temporarily, under threat.

On 18 April more Cold War stories were in the news with Captain Joseph P. Kaufmann of the USAF being sentenced to twenty years' hard labour for giving secrets to the East Germans. On the same day warrants were issued for the arrest of former British diplomats Burgess and Maclean who had 'disappeared' or more likely 'sneaked off' behind the Iron Curtain back in 1951.

On 21 April the government announced the latest unemployment figures, which were down by 3,128 to 438,673. Three days later the newspapers revealed the national scandal and 'serious menace to public health' that was Pirate Hairdressers. The president of the hairdressers' trade organisation, Wallace F. Scowcroft of Levenshulme, was quoted as speaking out against 'unscrupulous partly trained men and women whose activities dishonour our ancient craft.' Presumably you could always tell a 'pirate hairdresser' because they used 'cut-throat' razors.

Moving south to Coventry the new cathedral designed by Sir Basil Spence was virtually complete when on 27 April the spire, which was made in Suffolk, was lowered onto the roof of the building by helicopter.

In France there was trouble on the streets of Paris and the police formed a special squad to deal with the *Blousons Noir* who were a sort of French Teddy Boy. Clashes between them and the police resulted in two deaths and several injuries.

Back in Ipswich it was another month of heady entertainment with the Twist Formation Team strutting or wriggling their stuff at the Ipswich Ballroom Dancing Studios. At the cinema, the Ritz in the Buttermarket stopped being the Ritz and became the ABC and was showing *Carry On Cruising*. If not in the mood for comedy the Odeon in Lloyds Avenue offered a stark contrast with *The Guns Of Navarone*.

On Friday 13 April there was an awful tragedy at the Foxhall Stadium when thirty-four-year-old Jack Unstead collided with Peter Vandenburg on the first bend in the first lap of his speedway race. He was thrown against a floodlight pylon and killed. Unstead had been a guest rider for the Witches in their match against Southampton; he was the first rider to be killed at Foxhall since speedway restarted in Ipswich in 1951.

The month ended with the Ipswich Carnival on 28 April, the same day as the final league game of the season. Coming up at the rear of the carnival procession were the Ipswich Lambretta Club on their shiny scooters.

And finally . . . Match No. 42
Saturday 28 April 1962
Venue: Portman Road
Ipswich Town 2–0 Aston Villa   Attendance: 28,932

Town's final match in their first ever season in the First Division of the Football League had arrived. Incredibly, they were top of the table. The simple facts were that if Town beat Aston Villa and Burnley failed to beat Chelsea, then Ipswich Town would be the league champions.

Town's team was unchanged for the fourth game in a row, it was same the team that Alf Ramsey had fielded in twenty-six of the season's forty-one other league matches. It was John Compton's fiftieth consecutive first team game.

Prior to the game the Aston Villa manager Joe Mercer had predicted that Burnley would become league champions and that his team would beat Ipswich Town – how very foolish of him! Inevitably a large crowd was expected for the game, although it was not all-ticket. Alf Ramsey and the Chief Constable appealed to fans, however, to get to Portman Road in good time and to pack together as tightly as possible, thus enabling everyone to see the game with the maximum of safety and comfort.

The line-ups were – Ipswich Town: Bailey; Carberry and Compton; Baxter, Nelson and Elsworthy; Stephenson, Moran, Crawford, Phillips and Leadbetter. Aston Villa: Sims; Lee and Aitken: Crowe, Sleeuwenhoek and

IPSWICH TOWN FOOTBALL CLUB COMPANY, LTD.

Directors:

JOHN C. COBBOLD (*Chairman*)   RT. HON. LORD CRANWORTH, K.G., M.C.
SIR CHARLES H. N. BUNBURY, BT.   CECIL J. ROBINSON
                                    NATHAN SHAW
CYRIL CATCHPOLE   ERNEST J. H. STEEL
ALISTAIR P. COBBOLD   MAJOR ALFRED D. R. TERRY

Secretary/Manager: A. E. RAMSEY.
Financial Secretary: W. A. GRAY.   *Telephone:* 51306.

TO-DAY'S GAME

No. 32,   Saturday, 28th April, 1962

IPSWICH TOWN
v.
ASTON VILLA

LEAGUE DIVISION I.
Kick-off 3 p.m.

FUTURE ATTRACTION AT PORTMAN ROAD
May   3   Suffolk Senior Cup Final
           Brantham v. Stowmarket   Kick-off 6.30 p.m.
TOUR MATCHES
May   1   T.S.V. Alemannia Aachen at
           Aachen   Kick-off 7.30 p.m.
May   3   Vejle Boldklub at Vejle   Kick-off 7.30 p.m.
May   9   K.S.V. Holstein at Kiel   Kick-off 7.30 p.m.
May 11   Offenbach Kickers at Offenbach Kick-off 6.30 p.m.

The final game of the season was on Saturday 28 April. If Town won and Burnley did not, then Ipswich Town would be the champions. The programme shows that whatever the result, three days later the team would be on tour in West Germany.

Deakin; MacEwan, Baker, Dougan, Thomson and Ewing. The referee was Mr
E. Crawford of Doncaster.

All that mattered in this game was that Town won, but for seventy minutes
there looked little prospect of that as chances were few and far between. Ted
Phillips had headed a Roy Stephenson cross past the far post but otherwise
the closest Town had come to taking the lead was after thirteen minutes when
Villa's England under-23 international Alan Deakin had sent a header towards
his own goal, forcing goalkeeper Sims to make a fingertip save. While Town
constantly pressured the Villa defence throughout the first half they were
unable to break through and were frequently caught offside. Roy Stephenson
looked dangerous for Town, supplying crosses and through-balls, but Villa
held firm and had a few chances of their own with Derek Dougan being put
through on goal only to be given offside and Larry Carberry being forced to
dispatch the ball narrowly past the post under pressure from Dougan.

Town fans could only have been a bit disappointed at half time with the
lack of a goal and although the sun shone for the start of the second half the
situation did not improve, with Villa beginning to gain control of the game.

With the likelihood of Town claiming the league championship seemingly
slipping further and further away as every moment passed, the game entered
its last twenty minutes. Then, on seventy-two minutes Billy Baxter was fouled
far out on the right-hand side of the field. Roy Stephenson took the free-kick
and swung the ball in goalwards. John Elsworthy, who had pushed up from
his half-back position, leapt for the ball as it came into the penalty area; he
outjumped his opponents and met the ball firmly with his head, sending
it thudding against the crossbar. As the ball rebounded back out into the
penalty area Ray Crawford threw himself headlong at it; he connected and
his header sent the ball into the net past a flat-footed Sims.

Now trailing, with little more than a quarter of an hour to play, Villa were
desperate for an equaliser and pushed forward. Four minutes later Town
were pinned back into their own now-packed penalty area, but managed
to clear the ball out to the half-way line where Ray Crawford provided their
only outlet. With Crawford was just one Villa defender, eighteen-year-old
John Sleeuwenhoek. Gathering the cleared ball Crawford controlled it and
bore down on the Aston Villa goal, but Sleeuwenhoek was in hot pursuit and
before Crawford was in a position to shoot he moved in and tackled him. The
opportunity appeared to have been lost but Crawford recovered quickly to
win the ball back again before taking one look up and smacking the ball into
the net past Sims.

In the remaining fourteen minutes there was still time for Phillips to have a
goal disallowed for offside and for Leadbetter to send an effort narrowly the
wrong side of a post, but otherwise that was the end of the story. With the
news that Burnley had failed to beat already-relegated Chelsea at Turf Moor
(it was a 1–1 draw) Ipswich Town had created history and had, against all the
odds, become the Football League Champions.

Action from the first half of that game at Portman Road versus Aston Villa. Ray Crawford worries Sims in the Villa goal (above) and Ted Phillips does likewise (below).

The other results for the final Saturday of the league programme went like this, and included the second 8–3 scoreline of the season:

Arsenal	2–0	Sheffield United
Birmingham City	2–3	Tottenham Hotspur
Bolton Wanderers	1–0	West Ham United
Burnley	1–1	Chelsea
Everton	8–3	Cardiff City
Fulham	2–0	Manchester United
Leicester City	2–1	Nottingham Forest
Manchester City	3–1	Blackburn Rovers
Sheffield Wednesday	3–2	Wolverhampton Wanderers
West Bromwich Albion	7–1	Blackpool

Unlike in the modern game, there was no edict from the League or Football Association saying that all games had to be played by the last Saturday of the season and so there were a handful of games played during the following week, the results of which were largely academic, but they produced these results:

Town's game at home to Aston Villa finished a short while before Burnley's game with Chelsea. Having won 2–0 Town had done what was required of them, but they still needed Burnley not to win to be sure they could not be caught as Burnley still had another game to play. Happily Chelsea belied their lowly position in the league table (twenty-second) and held Burnley to a 1–1 draw. The cover of the Burnley programme for 1961/62 season shows a Turf Moor ground which has since been completely rebuilt.

30 April
Leicester City   2–3   Tottenham Hotspur
Sheffield Wednesday   4–0   Burnley
West Ham United   4–2   Fulham

1 May
Arsenal   2–3   Everton
Aston Villa   2–2   Cardiff City

The final league table for Division One therefore ended up like this:

	P	W	D	L	F	A	Pts	Goal Ave.
Ipswich Town C	42	24	8	10	93	67	56	1.39
Burnley	42	21	11	10	101	67	53	1.51
Tottenham Hotspur	42	21	10	11	88	69	52	1.28
Everton	42	20	11	11	88	54	51	1.63
Sheffield United	42	19	9	14	61	69	47	0.88
Sheffield Wednesday	42	20	6	16	72	58	46	1.24
Aston Villa	42	18	8	16	65	56	44	1.16
West Ham United	42	17	10	15	76	82	44	0.93
West Bromwich Albion	42	15	13	14	83	67	43	1.24
Arsenal	42	16	11	15	71	72	43	0.99
Bolton Wanderers	42	16	10	16	62	66	42	0.94
Manchester City	42	17	7	18	78	81	41	0.96
Blackpool	42	15	11	16	70	75	41	0.93
Leicester City	42	17	6	19	72	71	40	1.01
Manchester United	42	15	9	18	72	75	39	0.96
Blackburn Rovers	42	14	11	17	50	58	39	0.86
Birmingham City	42	14	10	18	65	81	38	0.80
Wolverhampton Wanderers	42	13	10	19	73	86	36	0.85
Nottingham Forest	42	13	10	19	63	79	36	0.80
Fulham	42	13	7	22	66	74	33	0.89
Cardiff City R	42	9	14	19	50	81	32	0.62
Chelsea R	42	9	10	23	63	94	28	0.67

9   The Players

During the course of the whole 1961/62 season manager Alf Ramsey called upon just seventeen players in competitive matches. Of those seventeen, Doug Millward played in a solitary League Cup game and saw no action in the league itself. The use of just sixteen players in a Championship-winning League season was a new record, beating Tottenham's previous record of seventeen, which had only been established the year before. It was a new record for Town, too, who had previously also not used fewer than seventeen players in a single league campaign. These were the players that Town called upon:

Roy Bailey
Born on 26 May 1932 in Epsom, Surrey, Roy was the fifth child in a family of thirteen children. He began his career at the age of fifteen with Tottenham juniors but signed as an amateur for Crystal Palace because they were so much closer to his home. Roy made his debut for Palace at the age of seventeen but did not play regularly until his National Service was completed. After joining Town from Crystal Palace in March 1956 he played a total of 348 games between April 1956 and September 1964. Roy was the first-choice goalkeeper for Ipswich almost as soon as he arrived at the club. He played in 37 of Town's 42 league games in the 1961/62 season, his place being covered by Wilf Hall in the other five fixtures. His first game for Town was in a 3–2 defeat at Carrow Road on 2 April 1956 and his last was a 4–1 League Cup defeat at Coventry on 23 September 1964. Roy later emigrated to South Africa. As well as being our Championship-winning goalie he has a lesser claim to fame as the father of the erstwhile Manchester United keeper Gary Bailey, who of course never won a medal like his dad's. Roy died in Johannesburg in April 1993.

Billy Baxter
Born on 23 April 1939 in Edinburgh, Billy Baxter played in Town's defence in 40 of their 42 league games. Billy had signed from Broxburn Athletic in June 1960 and played 459 games before being sold to West Bromwich Albion by Bobby Robson in January 1971. Baxter's debut for Town was as a left-back in a 3–0 victory over Norwich City on 27 December 1960. His final appearance for Town was on 23 January 1971 in a 1–1 draw in the FA Cup fourth round at The Hawthorns. During the course of the 1961/62 season Billy was undertaking his National Service in the Army, joining the Royal Engineers based in Farnborough. As well as playing for Ipswich, Baxter was also a regular in the Army football team, playing in the Kentish Cup and in inter-services games. Billy Baxter died in Dunfermline in May 2009.

Larry Carberry

Born in Liverpool on 18 January 1936, the second of five children, right-back Larry Carberry played in every league game in the 1961/62 season. Although he had previously signed for Everton as an amateur, Town were Carberry's first professional club and, having signed in May 1956, he went on to play 285 games before joining Swindon Town in October 1964. Ipswich signed Larry having seen him in action against Bury Town for his Army regiment, the King's, while he completed his National Service in Bury St Edmunds. Larry initially signed for Town as an amateur and had attracted interest from various other clubs including Norwich, Stoke City and Liverpool. His Town debut was in a 4–0 league win at home to Queen's Park Rangers on 3 November 1956 and his farewell was on 31 October 1964 in a 3–1 defeat away at Swindon.

John Compton

The eldest in a family of five and born on 27 August 1937 in Poplar, east London, John Compton played in all but the first three of Town's forty-two league matches in the Championship season. He came in to the side as cover for Ken Malcolm who had been struck down with sciatica. Originally a midfielder, Alf Ramsey successfully converted him into Town's left-back for the season. Compton's father had been an amateur player with Millwall and John himself was offered a trial at Charlton before joining Chelsea at the age of sixteen. His league debut was made for Chelsea at Blackpool in a Division One match when he was just seventeen years old. Having signed for Town from Chelsea in July 1960 for a fee of £4,000, Compton made his debut on 5 November 1960 in a 3–2 defeat at Luton. He went on to play 131 times before moving on to Wolverhampton Wanderers in April 1964, his final Town game being in a 1–0 league win over Wolves at Portman Road on 14 April 1964.

Ray Crawford

Born on 13 July 1937 in Portsmouth, Crawford was the eldest of four children. He played for Portsmouth Schoolboys and then in the Combined Services team while on National Service. It was his National Service, in which he served in Malaysia that earned him the nickname 'jungle boy'. Ray signed as a professional for Pompey in October 1956 and made his debut for them in a Division One match versus Burnley at Fratton Park on the opening day of the 1957/58 season. In just nineteen games he scored nine goals for Pompey but missed three months of the season with a broken ankle. In the summer of 1958 Pompey sacked their manager Eddie Lever and supposedly his final words to the directors as he left Fratton Park were, 'Whatever you do, don't sell Ray Crawford.' Predictably, three games into the 1958/59 season Crawford was sold to Ipswich by the new Pompey manager, Freddie Cox,

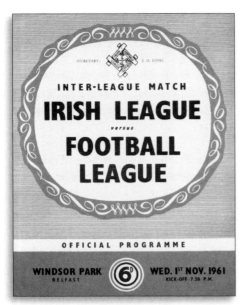

Ray Crawford was the top scorer in Football League Division One for the 1961/62 season with 33 league goals. His clear supremacy over the strikers of other teams was rewarded in November by his selection for the Football League in a representative match against the Irish League at Windsor Park, Belfast. The English Football League won 6–1 and Ray Crawford scored two of the goals.

Ray Crawford's selection for the Football League XI was to presage his selection for the full England team in the next international fixture at Wembley, a Home International fixture versus Northern Ireland on 22 November. Although Wembley had floodlights, this game kicked off at 2.30 on a Wednesday afternoon. The game ended in a 1–1 draw with England's goal being scored by Bobby Charlton, although Ray Crawford had provided him with the 'assist'.

for just £6,000. Pompey's loss was of course Ipswich Town's gain. Centre forward Crawford missed just one league game during the Championship season (the 5–0 away defeat at Old Trafford) and was Town's top scorer with 33 goals. After making representative appearances for the Football League XI during the 1961/62 season, Crawford was then also called up to play for England, appearing in the Home International game against Northern Ireland and for a match versus Austria, against whom he scored in a 3–1 win.

He therefore became the first Ipswich Town player to represent England. After signing for Wolverhampton Wanderers for £40,000 in September 1963, Crawford rejoined Town from West Bromwich Albion in March 1966 before

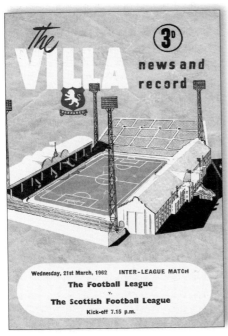

In March of 1962 Ray Crawford was once again selected to represent the Football League, this time in a match against the Scottish Football League at Villa Park. The Football League lost this match by four goals to three and Ray Crawford did not score. The design of the programme for this match was the same as that for Aston Villa's own fixtures. Villa Park proved not to be a happy hunting ground for Ray Crawford during the Championship season as Town lost 3–0 there in the league and he missed the League Cup win there in November because he was with the England squad.

Once again Ray Crawford's call-up to represent the Football League presaged his call up to the full England team and he earned his second cap in the 3–1 win over Austria. Despite scoring in this match Ray Crawford never played for England again, with the selectors incredibly preferring to take Alan Peacock, who had scored 24 goals in the Second Division for Middlesbrough, to the World Cup finals in Chile in the summer of 1962. As usual, England flopped.

leaving again, this time for Charlton Athletic in March 1969, having played a total of 354 games in his two stints at the club and having scored 228 goals. He went on to play for Colchester United, famously scoring twice in their legendary 3–2 FA Cup win over Leeds United in 1971. Ray went on to play for Durban City in South Africa and was coach at Brighton & Hove Albion when Brian Clough was manager there. Late in 1973 he became youth team coach back at Pompey and then assistant to manager Jimmy Dickinson until January 1978. Ray later worked for a wholesalers in Portsmouth alongside the author's mother-in-law's next-door neighbour.

Dermot Curtis

Born in Dublin on 26 August 1932, centre forward Curtis had signed from Bristol City in August 1958. He played four times in the 1961/62 season, filling in once for Roy Stephenson, once for Ray Crawford and twice wearing the number ten shirt of Ted Phillips. He began his career with an Irish club called St Finbars when about fourteen years old. He then moved to League of Ireland club Shelbourne and in 1956 joined Bristol City. Curtis was an Eire international and had played for his country fifteen times by the end of the 1961/62 season. After a total of 43 appearances for Town, in which he scored 18 goals, Dermot Curtis signed for Aston Villa in May 1963. He died in Exeter on 1 November 2008.

John Elsworthy

Born in Nantyderry on 26 July 1931, Elsworthy was spotted playing for the RAF while completing his National Service at Mildenhall. A good cricketer as well as a footballer, Elsworthy had been offered a trial for Glamorgan. He initially signed for Town from Newport County as an amateur in May 1949 and made his debut in a 4–0 home defeat to Notts County on 27 December the same year. He missed just one league game (the 1–0 win at home to Cardiff City) in the Championship-winning season. Wearing the number six shirt, wing-half Elsworthy scored two goals in the course of the season. Described as a 'gentle giant' Elsworthy measured 6ft 3in and by the time he retired from football in 1965 he had made 435 first team appearances for Town, his last being on 19 September 1964 in a 4–1 home defeat to Bolton Wanderers. During his time at Portman Road Elsworthy gathered a record haul of two Division Three (South) Championship medals, one Second Division Championship medal and of course one First Division Championship medal. John Elsworthy died in Ipswich on 3 May 2009.

Wilf Hall

Born on 14 October 1934 in Haydock, keeper Wilf made just five league appearances during the course of the season, deputising for the injured Roy Bailey. Sadly despite sterling performances from Wilf the team failed to keep a single clean sheet in any of these games and Town won only one of them, versus Sheffield Wednesday at Hillsborough. Wilf signed from Stoke City on 1 June 1960 having played over 100 first team games for the Potters since joining them at the age of eighteen. He made his debut against Derby County on 27 August in a 4–1 victory but in total played only 19 games for Town, always being the 'understudy' to first-choice Roy Bailey. Wilf left for West Bromwich Albion in 1963 having made his last appearance for Town against the Throstles on 9 March in a 6–1 defeat at The Hawthorns.

Jimmy Leadbetter

One of the oldest players in the team, Leadbetter was born in Edinburgh on 28 July 1928. He was known as 'Sticks' at Portman Road because of his spindly legs and light frame, but the national press applied all sorts of unflattering descriptions to him. In the *Observer* Clement Freud wrote of 'pale, venerable Leadbetter,' while Tony Pawson referred to Jimmy as, 'frail, worried and slow.' Elsewhere he was described as looking like Steptoe's father and in his biography of Alf Ramsey, Dave Bowler describes Jimmy as having the pace of an injured snail. Jimmy began his professional career in England with Chelsea in 1949 having moved south from Scottish Junior club Armandale Thistle. But in three seasons Jimmy played only three first team games (all in the space of four days over Easter 1952) and when Ted Drake became Chelsea manager Jimmy was swiftly transferred to Brighton & Hove Albion as the 'makeweight' in a part exchange deal that saw Johnny McNichol move to Chelsea. Down at the Goldstone Ground Jimmy fared much better than he had at Chelsea, playing 120 times for the Seagulls before asking for a move. He took a cut in wages to sign for Town in June 1955 and made his debut in a 1–0 home win over Bournemouth on 8 October that same year. He had been an inside forward but was converted to deep-lying winger by Alf Ramsey. Jimmy missed just one game during the Championship season (versus Leicester at home) when his number eleven shirt went to Aled Owen. In total Jimmy played an impressive 375 times for Town scoring 49 goals, eight of them during the Championship season. He made his final appearance for Town in a 5–0 FA Cup defeat at Tottenham on 30 January 1965. He left Town the following June but continued to play until he was forty-three years old for Sudbury Town, a club he also managed. Jimmy was one of three Town players to win Division Three (South), Division Two and Division One Championship medals with Town. He died in Edinburgh on 18 July 2006.

Ken Malcolm

Born in Aberdeen on 25 July 1926 and signed from Arbroath in July 1954, Ken was the oldest member of the team and had played some 280 games for Town by April 1962, a total exceeded by only five other players at the time. Ken made his debut against Hull City on 4 September 1954 in a 4–2 defeat at Boothferry Park. In the 1961/62 season Ken wore the number three shirt in the first three games. Unfortunately for him, however, after missing the home game with Burnley on 29 August due to a leg injury, three days later he was admitted to hospital with sciatica. In Ken's absence John Compton took up the number three shirt and made it his own, right up until he left the club in 1964. Ken's first English professional club had been Wolverhampton Wanderers, but his time there had been curtailed by a career-threatening injury. After the Championship win, Ken only played eighteen more times for Town before retiring at the end of the 1963/64 season, his final game being on 9 March 1963 in a 4–1 defeat at West Bromwich. Ken Malcolm died in Ipswich on 23 May 2006.

Doug Millward

Born in Sheffield on 31 July 1931, Doug did not feature in any of Ipswich's league matches in the 1961/62 season but played in a League Cup second round replay at home to Swansea Town; he wore the number two shirt in place of Larry Carberry although he was a forward. In total he played 156 times for Town scoring 36 goals. He signed from Southampton in June 1955, waiting until 2 April 1956 for his debut in a 3–2 reversal at Carrow Road. Doug's farewell performance was on 9 March 1963 in a 6–1 trouncing at West Bromwich, after which he left for Poole Town in June 1963. He died on 23 October 2000.

Doug Moran

Born in Musselburgh on 29 July 1934, Doug was Alf Ramsey's only addition to the Division Two Championship-winning side of the previous season. He was Town's record signing at the time. He was signed from Falkirk, who had just been promoted to Scottish League Division One, after finishing second in the Second Division behind Stirling Albion. The fee was £12,000. He was ever-present in the Town team during the 1961/62 season. Doug began his football career at the age of seventeen, signing as a part-timer for Hibernian for whom he played just ten first team games. He was then loaned to Falkirk and signed for them during the close season in 1956 for a fee of £1,500. Within twelve months he had won a Scottish Cup winners' medal and indeed scored the winning goal against Kilmarnock. At Portman Road the other players gave him the nickname of 'Dixie'. Alf Ramsey was extremely pleased to have signed Moran and was quoted as saying that he could not have found a player so useful to the club if he had had £30,000 to spend.

Andy Nelson

Born at Custom House in east London on 5 July 1935, the fifth of eight children, Andy Nelson was the team captain. He had signed from West Ham United, where he had been a part-timer, in May 1959, making his debut on 22 August against Huddersfield Town. He was an ever-present in the side in the 1961/62 season, playing in all ten league and FA Cup games as well as the forty-two league matches. A half-back, he did not score in any of his fifty-two games that season or indeed in any of his 215 games for Town. He left the club in September 1964 when he joined Leyton Orient, his final game being a 2–1 defeat against Norwich City on 5 September 1964. He later went on to become manager of both Gillingham and Charlton Athletic . . . though not at the same time.

Aled Owen

Born in Cae Ysgawen on Anglesey, North Wales, on 7 January 1934, Owen was a winger who began his professional career at the age of nineteen with Tottenham Hotspur when Alf Ramsey was still a player there. He signed for Ipswich from Tottenham Hotspur in July 1958 making his debut against Sunderland in a 2–0 victory at Roker Park on 20 September that year. He played just one league game in the Championship season taking Jimmy Leadbetter's number eleven shirt for the Boxing Day win over Leicester City. His last game for Town was a 1–1 draw in the FA Cup versus Luton Town in that same season, but he did not leave Town until the end of the following season when he returned to the 'land of his fathers', signing for Wrexham. In five years he had played 35 times for Town scoring three goals.

Ted Phillips

The only 'local' player in the entire team, Ted Phillips was born in Leiston on 21 August 1933. Town had signed Phillips from Leiston back in December of 1953 and he had therefore been involved in both of the Division Three (South) Championship wins, the Second Division Championship win and the Division One title success – although he did not get a medal in the first Division Three success in 1954 because he had only played three matches. Ted actually made his debut in the 1953/54 season on 3 March at Watford. A powerful, 6ft 1in inside forward with reputedly the hardest shot in football at the time, Phillips holds the record as the scorer of the most goals for Town in a single season; 46 in Cup and league in 1956/57. Ironically, for a player whose shots were always likely to injure goalkeepers who got in the way, he started out in local football in goal. In the Championship campaign he netted twenty-eight times in forty matches, plus another eight in the ten Cup games. Ted was the club's penalty-taker, scoring twenty-five in twenty-eight attempts in his time at the club, eight of his successes coming in the 1961/62 season, five of them in the league. In total Phillips played 295 games, scoring 181 goals before moving to Leyton Orient in March 1964 having played his last game, a 4–0 defeat on 22 February at Chelsea.

Reg Pickett

The second eldest team member, Pickett was born in Bareilly, India, on 6 January 1927. Wing-half Reg had signed from Portsmouth at the close of the 1956/57 season. Reg was the only member of the squad to already have a Championship medal, which he won with Portsmouth, making fourteen appearances in their triumphant 1949/50 season when in fact they retained the title having won it the previous season also. Reg was an accomplished player capable of operating in virtually every position on the field and for Pompey he played both at wing-half and as a forward. He captained Town from November 1957 to the end of the 1959/60 season. In the title-winning season Reg played just three league games for Town, wearing Billy Baxter's number four shirt in the victories away at Leicester City and at home to Wolverhampton Wanderers in March, and taking on the number six shirt of John Elsworthy in the home win over Cardiff City in mid-April. After a total of 148 games and four goals Reg left for Stevenage Town at the end of the following season. He now lives in Portsmouth.

Roy Stephenson

Born in Crook, County Durham, on 27 May 1932, right-winger Stephenson missed just a single game (the 4–1 home win over Manchester United) in the Championship season; Dermot Curtis filled in to wear the number seven shirt on that occasion. Scorer of seven goals during the season, Stephenson had been signed by Alf Ramsey from Leicester City in July 1960. Roy had begun his career at Burnley, joining the ground staff at the age of sixteen and then becoming a part-time professional. He went on to play more than 100 First Division games for the Clarets scoring a creditable 28 goals before moving to Rotherham United for a fee of £4,500. But a year later he moved back to Lancashire to join Blackburn Rovers for whom he played in the 1958 FA Cup semi-final against the eventual winners Bolton Wanderers. Roy then signed for Leicester City for a fee of £8,000 but soon moved on to Ipswich, making his debut on 13 September 1960 in a 4–0 win over Brighton & Hove Albion at Portman Road. He stayed with Town until June 1965 when, after a total on 163 games, in which he scored 26 goals, he signed for Lowestoft Town. His final game for Town was on 31 October 1964 in a 3–1 defeat at Swindon. Roy Stephenson died in February 2000.

Other Staff

Jimmy Forsyth (Trainer)

Born in Armadale, West Lothian, on 18 October 1904, Jimmy played over 350 League games for Portsmouth, Gillingham and Millwall. He served his 500th consecutive match as Ipswich first team trainer during the course of the 1961/62 season having joined the club at the end of the 1949/50 season. As a player Jimmy had been in the successful Millwall side that reached the FA Cup semi-final in 1937 and won promotion to the Second Division in 1938. Prior to joining Town, Jimmy had been assistant trainer at Millwall, a position he had held since 1945. Jimmy Forsyth retired from football in 1971 and died in 1982.

Trainer Jimmy Forsyth, who had served the club since the 1949/50 season, is pictured with a group of players on the practice pitch at Portman Road, behind what is now the Britannia Stand. He appears to be explaining what a football looks like. If they hadn't arrived by bicycle some of the players would have travelled to training on the bus and coincidentally the Corporation bus garage can be seen on the left.

Charlie Cowie (Assistant Trainer)

Born in Falkirk on 23 April 1907, Charlie had played as centre-half for Town in the 1930s before being appointed assistant trainer in 1946. He had been one of Ipswich's first professional players back in 1936 and played sixty-six times for Town in the three years before the outbreak of the Second World War. Prior to joining Town Charlie had played for both Barrow and Heart of Midlothian. Charlie Cowie died in 1971.

10   Statistics

Final League Table

			Home						Away			
	P	W	D	L	F	A	W	D	L	F	A	Pts
Ipswich Town	**42**	**17**	**2**	**2**	**58**	**28**	**7**	**6**	**8**	**35**	**39**	**56**
Burnley	42	14	4	3	57	26	7	7	7	44	41	53
Tottenham Hotspur	42	14	4	3	59	34	7	6	8	29	35	52
Everton	42	17	2	2	64	21	3	9	9	24	33	51
Sheffield United	42	13	5	3	37	23	6	4	11	24	46	47
Sheffield Wednesday	42	14	4	3	47	23	6	2	13	25	35	46
Aston Villa	42	13	5	3	45	20	5	3	13	20	36	44
West Ham United	42	11	6	4	49	37	6	4	11	27	45	44
West Bromwich Albion	42	10	7	4	50	23	5	6	10	33	44	43
Arsenal	42	9	6	6	39	31	7	5	9	32	41	43
Bolton Wanderers	42	11	7	3	35	22	5	3	13	27	44	42
Manchester City	42	11	3	7	46	38	6	4	11	32	43	41
Blackpool	42	10	4	7	41	30	5	7	9	29	45	41
Leicester City	42	12	2	7	38	27	5	4	12	34	44	40
Manchester United	42	10	3	8	44	31	5	6	10	28	44	39
Blackburn Rovers	42	10	6	5	33	22	4	5	12	17	36	39
Birmingham City	42	9	6	6	37	35	5	4	12	28	46	38
Wolverhampton Wanderers	42	8	7	6	38	34	5	3	13	35	52	36
Nottingham Forest	42	12	4	5	39	23	1	6	14	24	56	36
Fulham	42	8	3	10	38	34	5	4	12	28	40	33
Cardiff City	**42**	**6**	**9**	**6**	**30**	**33**	**3**	**5**	**13**	**20**	**48**	**32**
Chelsea	**42**	**7**	**7**	**7**	**34**	**29**	**2**	**3**	**16**	**29**	**65**	**28**

Sequences
Most consecutive defeats – 2. Games 2 and 3
Most consecutive draws – 2. Games 33 and 34
Most consecutive wins – 4. Games 4 to 7
Longest run of games without a win – 3. Games 1 to 3 and 8 to 10
Longest run of games without a defeat –10. Games 27 to 36
Longest run of games without a draw – 13. Games 16 to 28

Summary of Results

No.	Date	H/A	Opp	Score	Att	Pts	Pos
1	19/8/61	A	Bolton Wanderers	0–0	16,708	1	13
2	22/8/61	A	Burnley	3–4	24,577	1	15
3	26/8/61	H	Manchester City	2–4	21,473	1	19
4	29/8/61	H	Burnley	6–2	23,835	3	11
5	2/9/61	A	West Bromwich Albion	3–1	19,016	5	9
6	5/9/61	H	Blackburn Rovers	2–1	24,928	7	6
7	9/9/61	H	Birmingham City	4–1	20,017	9	5
8	16/9/61	A	Everton	2–5	35,259	9	7
9	18/9/61	A	Blackburn Rovers	2–2	19,904	10	6
10	23/9/61	H	Fulham	2–4	23,050	10	8
11	30/9/61	A	Sheffield Wednesday	4–1	26,565	12	6
12	7/10/61	H	West Ham United	4–2	28,059	14	4
13	14/10/61	A	Sheffield United	1–2	22,194	14	6
14	21/10/61	H	Tottenham Hotspur	3–2	28,778	16	4
15	28/10/61	A	Blackpool	1–1	19,773	17	4
16	4/11/61	H	Nottingham Forest	1–0	19,068	19	3
17	11/11/61	A	Wolverhampton Wanderers	0–2	21,711	19	5
18	18/11/61	H	Manchester United	4–1	25,755	21	3
19	25/11/61	A	Cardiff City	3–0	22,823	23	2
20	2/12/61	H	Chelsea	5–2	22,726	25	2
21	9/12/61	A	Aston Villa	0–3	31,924	25	3
22	16/12/61	H	Bolton Wanderers	2–1	16,587	27	2
23	23/12/62	A	Manchester City	0–3	18,376	27	5
24	26/12/61	H	Leicester City	1–0	18,146	29	4
25	13/1/62	H	West Bromwich Albion	3–0	18,378	31	3
26	20/1/62	A	Birmingham City	1–3	26,968	31	4
27	3/2/62	H	Everton	4–2	22,572	33	2
28	10/2/62	A	Fulham	2–1	25,209	35	3
29	24/2/62	A	West Ham United	2–2	27,762	36	3
30	3/3/62	H	Sheffield United	4–0	20,158	38	2
31	9/3/62	H	Sheffield Wednesday	2–1	23,713	40	2
32	14/3/62	A	Tottenham Hotspur	3–1	51,098	42	2
33	17/3/62	H	Blackpool	1–1	22,450	43	2
34	24/3/62	A	Nottingham Forest	1–1	26,053	44	2
35	28/3/62	A	Leicester City	2–0	19,068	46	2
36	31/3/62	H	Wolverhampton Wanderers	3–2	23,153	48	1
37	7/4/62	A	Manchester United	0–5	24,976	48	2
38	14/4/62	H	Cardiff City	1–0	17,693	50	1
39	20/4/62	H	Arsenal	2–2	30,649	51	2
40	21/4/62	A	Chelsea	2–2	28,462	52	1
41	23/4/62	A	Arsenal	3–0	44,694	54	1
42	28/4/62	H	Aston Villa	2–0	28,932	56	1

Average League Attendances in Division One for 1961/62
The clubs are listed in order of the highest average home league attendances. Despite being the club with only the sixteenth highest average attendance at home, Ipswich were the fifth most popular attraction away from home. However, it must be taken into account that the range between highest and lowest average away attendances was only 18,214 compared to 29,487 for home averages and only three teams (Tottenham Hotspur, Manchester United and Burnley) drew average crowds of more than 30,000 for away games.

	Club	League Pos	Home Average	Away Average
1	Tottenham Hotspur	3	45,544	39,418
2	Everton	4	41,801	26,179
3	Arsenal	10	34,422	27,093
4	Manchester United	15	33,330	33,585
5	Aston Villa	7	32,648	25,367
6	Sheffield Wednesday	6	29,794	25,370
7	Burnley	2	27,171	31,681
8	Chelsea	22	27,013	25,525
9	Manchester City	12	25,626	24,868
10	West Ham United	8	25,372	26,056
11	Wolverhampton Wanderers	18	24,825	26,836
12	Fulham	20	24,456	24,745
13	Birmingham City	17	23,583	23,962
14	Nottingham Forest	19	23,309	24,150
15	Sheffield United	5	22,953	24,448
16	Ipswich Town	1	22,835	26,920
17	West Bromwich Albion	9	21,975	23,962
18	Cardiff City	21	19,731	21,204
19	Leicester City	14	19,454	22,887
20	Blackpool	13	18,618	25,135
21	Bolton Wanderers	11	17,512	23,300
22	Blackburn Rovers	16	15,857	25,144

Ipswich Town's average home gate for the previous season when they won the Second Division championship was 15,095. Average attendances at Portman Road therefore increased by more than 50 per cent in the Championship season.

Highest Away Attendance: 51,098 at White Hart Lane versus Tottenham
   Hotspur, Wednesday 14 March 1962
Highest Home Attendance: 30,649 versus Arsenal, Friday 20 April 1962
   (Good Friday)
Lowest Away Attendance: 16,708 at Burnden Park versus Bolton
   Wanderers, Saturday 19 August 1961 (opening game of the season)
Lowest Home Attendance: 16,587 versus Bolton Wanderers,
   Saturday 16 December 1961

The average gate for the whole division was 26,106.

Penalties Received

Town were awarded five penalty kicks in league matches during the course
of the season. All five were taken and scored by Ted Phillips and they were
as follows:

18 September v Blackburn Rovers at Ewood Park (result 2–2)
24 February v West Ham United at Upton Park (result 2–2)
31 March v Wolverhampton Wanderers at Portman Road (result 3–2)
20 April v Arsenal at Portman Road (result 2–2)
21 April v Chelsea at Stamford Bridge (result 2–2)

Penalties Conceded

Two penalty kicks were conceded by Ipswich in league games during the
1961/62 season. The first was on 5 September 1961 when Brian Douglas of
Blackburn Rovers scored his team's only goal in their 2–1 defeat at Portman
Road. The second penalty was taken by Calvin Palmer of Nottingham Forest
in the match at Portman Road on 4 November 1961, but his kick was saved
by Roy Bailey and Town won 1–0.

Own Goals

Only one player from another team was generous enough to score for
the Town during the course of the league season; this was Barry Betts of
Manchester City, who scored in the thirty-fourth minute of the game at
Portman Road on 26 August. City were winning 2–0 at the time and went on
to win 4–2.

Town scored two goals for the opposition through the course of the league
season. John Elsworthy managed to score an own goal for Burnley in the 6–2
victory at Portman Road on Tuesday 29 August and Billy Baxter scored for
Birmingham City in Town's 3–1 defeat at St Andrews on 20 January.

Goalscorers

Only six players scored league goals for Town during the season and very nearly two-thirds of Town's ninety-three league goals were scored by just two players, Ray Crawford and Ted Phillips.

	League	FA Cup	League Cup	Total
Ray Crawford	33	1	3	37
Ted Phillips	28	3	5	36
Doug Moran	14	1	3	18
Jimmy Leadbetter	8	1	1	10
Roy Stephenson	7	2	2	11
John Elsworthy	2	1	0	3
Own Goals	1	0	0	1
TOTAL	93	9	14	116

Ray Crawford was equal top goalscorer with Derek Kevan of West Bromwich Albion for the whole of Division One. Ray Charnley of Blackpool was the Division's third highest goalscorer with Ted Phillips the fourth highest.

Ray Crawford was the nation's top goalscorer when all competitions were taken into account. He led Ray Charnley by a single goal, while Ted Phillips was the third highest goal scorer in all competitions.

Hat-tricks

Ray Crawford was the only Town player to score a hat-trick in the Championship season. He scored this in the 5–2 victory over Chelsea on 2 December 1961.

Two players from opposing teams scored hat-tricks against Town; these being Derek Temple of Everton in the 5–2 defeat at Goodison Park on 16 September 1961 and Albert Quixall of Manchester United in the 5–0 defeat at Old Trafford on 7 April 1962.

Appearances

The striking feature of Ipswich Town's 1961/62 season as far as player appearances was concerned was the fact that they used only sixteen players in their forty-two league matches; a record low for the club and indeed for the whole Football League. Three players featured in all forty-two league games while six more missed just two games or less. One player, Ken Malcolm, suffered an injury after just three matches and did not play another league game all season but his replacement, John Compton, played all the remaining thirty-nine games; such was the consistency and continuity in the Ipswich Town team in their Championship-winning season.

The table that follows shows the number of appearances of each player in the league and, in addition, the two cup competitions:

Summary of first team appearances:

Player	League	FA Cup	League Cup	Total
Roy Bailey (GK)	37	4	3	44
Wilf Hall (GK)	5	1	2	8
Ken Malcolm	3	-	-	3
John Compton	39	5	5	49
Larry Carberry	42	5	4	51
Bill Baxter	40	5	5	50
Reg Pickett	3	-	-	3
Andy Nelson	42	5	5	52
John Elsworthy	41	5	5	51
Roy Stephenson	41	5	4	50
Dermot Curtis	4	-	1	5
Doug Moran	42	5	4	51
Ray Crawford	41	5	4	50
Ted Phillips	40	5	5	50
Jimmy Leadbetter	41	3	5	49
Aled Owen	1	2	1	4

The following table shows in which league games each player appeared.

Summary of team line-ups in league matches

Match	Date	Venue	Opponents	Score	Bailey	Hall	Carberry	Malcolm	Compton	Baxter	Pickett	Nelson (capt)	Elsworthy	Stephenson	Curtis	Moran	Crawford	Phillips	Leadbetter	Owen
1	19/08/1961	A	Bolton Wanderers	0–0	1		2	3		4		5	6	7		8	9	10	11	
2	22/08/1961	A	Burnley	3–4	1		2	3		4		5	6	7		8	9	10	11	
3	26/08/1961	H	Manchester City	2–4	1		2	3		4		5	6	7		8	9	10	11	
4	29/08/1961	H	Burnley	6–2	1		2		3	4		5	6	7		8	9	10	11	
5	02/09/1961	A	West Bromwich Albion	3–1	1		2		3	4		5	6	7		8	9	10	11	
6	05/09/1961	H	Blackburn Rovers	2–1	1		2		3	4		5	6	7		8	9	10	11	
7	09/09/1961	H	Birmingham City	4–1	1		2		3	4		5	6	7		8	9	10	11	
8	16/09/1961	A	Everton	2–5		1	2		3	4		5	6	7		8	9	10	11	
9	18/09/1961	A	Blackburn Rovers	2–2		1	2		3	4		5	6	7		8	9	10	11	
10	23/09/1961	H	Fulham	2–4		1	2		3	4		5	6	7		8	9	10	11	
11	30/09/1961	A	Sheffield Wednesday	4–1		1	2		3	4		5	6	7		8	9	10	11	
12	07/10/1961	H	West Ham United	4–2	1		2		3	4		5	6	7		8	9	10	11	
13	14/10/1961	A	Sheffield United	1–2	1		2		3	4		5	6	7		8	9	10	11	

Match	Date	Venue	Opponents	Score	Bailey	Hall	Carberry	Malcolm	Compton	Baxter	Pickett	Nelson (capt)	Elsworthy	Stephenson	Curtis	Moran	Crawford	Phillips	Leadbetter	Owen
14	21/10/1961	H	Tottenham Hotspur	3–2	1		2		3	4		5	6	7		8	9	10	11	
15	28/10/1961	A	Blackpool	1–1	1		2		3	4		5	6	7		8	9	10	11	
16	04/11/1961	H	Nottingham Forest	1–0	1		2		3	4		5	6	7		8	9	10	11	
17	11/11/1961	A	Wolverhampton Wanderers	0–2	1		2		3	4		5	6	7		8	9	10	11	
18	18/11/1961	H	Manchester United	4–1	1		2		3	4		5	6		7	8	9	10	11	
19	25/11/1961	A	Cardiff City	3–0	1		2		3	4		5	6	7		8	9	10	11	
20	02/12/1961	H	Chelsea	5–2	1		2		3	4		5	6	7		8	9	10	11	
21	09/12/1961	A	Aston Villa	0–3	1		2		3	4		5	6	7		8	9	10	11	
22	16/12/1961	H	Bolton Wanderers	2–1	1		2		3	4		5	6	7		8	9	10	11	
23	23/12/1962	A	Manchester City	0–3	1		2		3	4		5	6	7		8	9	10	11	
24	26/12/1961	H	Leicester City	1–0	1		2		3	4		5	6	7		8	9	10		11
25	13/01/1962	H	West Bromwich Albion	3–0	1		2		3	4		5	6	7		8	9	10	11	
26	20/01/1962	A	Birmingham City	1–3		1	2		3	4		5	6	7		8	9	10	11	
27	03/02/1962	H	Everton	4–1	1		2		3	4		5	6	7		8	9	10	11	
28	10/02/1962	A	Fulham	2–1	1		2		3	4		5	6	7		8	9	10	11	
29	24/02/1962	A	West Ham United	2–2	1		2		3	4		5	6	7		8	9	10	11	
30	03/03/1962	H	Sheffield United	4–0	1		2		3	4		5	6	7		8	9	10	11	
31	09/03/1962	H	Sheffield Wednesday	2–1	1		2		3	4		5	6	7		8	9	10	11	
32	14/03/1962	A	Tottenham Hotspur	3–1	1		2		3	4		5	6	7		8	9	10	11	
33	17/03/1962	H	Blackpool	1–1	1		2		3	4		5	6	7		8	9	10	11	
34	24/03/1962	A	Nottingham Forest	1–1	1		2		3	4		5	6	7	10	8	9		11	
35	28/03/1962	A	Leicester City	2–0	1		2		3		4	5	6	7	10	8	9		11	
36	31/03/1962	H	Wolverhampton Wanderers	3–2	1		2		3		4	5	6	7		8	9	10	11	
37	07/04/1962	A	Manchester United	0–5	1		2		3	4		5	6	7	9	8		10	11	
38	14/04/1962	H	Cardiff City	1–0	1		2		3	4	6	5		7		8	9	10	11	
39	20/04/1962	H	Arsenal	2–2	1		2		3	4		5	6	7		8	9	10	11	
40	21/04/1962	A	Chelsea	2–2	1		2		3	4		5	6	7		8	9	10	11	
41	23/04/1962	A	Arsenal	3–0	1		2		3	4		5	6	7		8	9	10	11	
42	28/04/1962	H	Aston Villa	2–0	1		2		3	4		5	6	7		8	9	10	11	

Debuts

Only one player made his League debut for Ipswich during the course of the 1961/62 season; this was Doug Moran who wore the number eight shirt in the opening game at Bolton and proceeded to play in every single league, League Cup and FA Cup match that season.

Farewell Appearances

One player, Aled Owen, made his final appearance for Town during the 1961/62 season. This was in the 1–1 draw against Luton Town in the FA Cup third round replay at Kenilworth Road on 10 January 1962. Although he did not leave the club until June 1963 this was his last first team game. Aled Owen's last league game had been the 1–0 home victory over Leicester City on Boxing Day 1961.

Comebacks & Cock-Ups

Of the ten league games that Town lost, they had taken the lead in just one of them, this being the home game versus Fulham on 23 September. This seems to indicate that Town were adept at not losing once they had gone ahead but also they were not that great at fighting back to win matches once they had gone behind.

There were six matches however, where they took the lead but failed to collect both points with the opposition managing to equalise. These were the 1–1 home draw against Blackpool; the 2–2 draw at Blackburn, the 1–1 draw at Blackpool, the 1–1 draw at Nottingham Forest and the 2–2 draws at Chelsea and at home to Arsenal, both of which saw Town trail by two goals before coming back to equalise.

Conversely, on four occasions Town managed to come back to win having gone behind; at home to Tottenham, Bolton, and Sheffield Wednesday and away at Fulham. There was just one match in which Town went ahead but failed to hang on to the lead with the game ending in a draw; this was the 2–2 draw at Blackburn, a 'see-saw' game in which Town took a one goal lead before trailing 2–1.

Doubles

Town beat five teams twice in the league: West Bromwich Albion (3–1 away and 3–0 at home), Cardiff City (3–0 away and 1–0 at home), Sheffield Wednesday (4–1 away and 2–1 at home), Tottenham Hotspur (3–2 at home and 3–1 away) and Leicester City (1–0 at home and 2–0 away). Incidentally, Ipswich became the first team to 'double' Tottenham for three seasons.

Only one side, Manchester City, took maximum points from Ipswich, winning 4–2 at Portman Road and 3–0 at Maine Road, but Town beat City in the League Cup.

Breakdown of Scorelines

Of their forty-two league matches, Town won twenty-four, drew eight and lost ten. There follows a breakdown of the various scorelines according to how often they occurred.

Draws:

0–0	One (away)
1–1	Three (one at home, two away)
2–2	Four (one at home, three way) – in all four of these games Ted Phillips scored a penalty.

Defeats:

2–0	One (away)
3–0	Two (away)
5–0	One (away)
2–1	One (away)
3–1	One (away)
4–2	Two (both at home)
5–2	One (away)
4–3	One (away)

Victories:

1–0	Three (all at home)
2–0	Two (one at home, one away)
2–1	Four (three at home, one away)
3–0	Three (one at home, two away)
3–1	Two (both away)
3–2	Two (one at home, one away)
4–0	One (home)
4–1	Three (two at home, one away)
4–2	Two (both at home)
5–2	One (at home)
6–2	One (at home)

Clean Sheets & Firing Blanks

Town kept ten clean sheets during the league season and seven of these were at Portman Road. They failed to score in five matches, all of which were away from home. Town's first game of the season, away to Bolton Wanderers, was their only goalless draw.

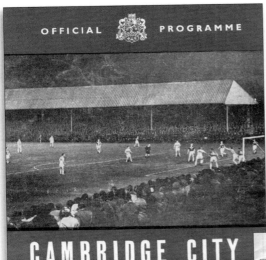

As well as playing forty-two league matches, five League Cup ties and five FA Cup ties Ipswich Town also played three friendly matches during the course of the 1961/62 season. Alf Ramsey fielded a largely first-choice XI in all three games. The illustration here shows the programme for a game at Cambridge City played in aid of the Haig Fund. Would a Premier League club even play such a game mid-season nowadays, let alone field a full-strength team?

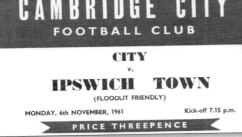

Other Matches

Aside from their successful forty-two-match league programme, Town played ten cup games, five in the League Cup and five in the FA Cup, plus three friendlies. In addition, they went on a three-match European Tour (well, Denmark and Germany) as soon as the season was complete where they beat both Vejle Boldklub and KSV Holstein 3–2, and lost 1–0 to Offenbach Kickers.

The following tables provide a summary of all the League Cup, FA Cup and friendly matches that Town played during the course of the 1961/62 season.

League Cup

	Date	Venue	Opponents	Attendance	Score	Roy Bailey	Wilf Hall	Carberry	Millward	Compton	Baxter	Nelson	Elsworthy	Stephenson	Owen	Moran	Crawford	Curtis	Phillips	Leadbetter
1st Round	11/9/61	H	Manchester City	14,919	4–2		1	2		3	4	5	6	7		8	9		10	11
2nd Round	3/10/61	A	Swansea Town	13,541	3–3	1		2	3	4	5	6	7		8	9			10	11
Replay	24/10/61	H	Swansea Town	11,010	3–2	1		2		3	4	5	6	7		8	9		10	11
3rd Round	21/11/61	A	Aston Villa	22,000	3–2	1		2		3	4	5	6		7	8		9	10	11
4th Round	11/12/61	A	Blackburn Rovers	11,071	1–4	1		2		3	4	5	6	7		8	9		10	11

FA Cup

	Date	Venue	Opponents	Attendance	Score	Roy Bailey	Wilf Hall	Carberry	Compton	Baxter	Nelson	Elsworthy	Stephenson	Moran	Crawford	Phillips	Leadbetter	Owen
1st Round	6/1/62	H	Luton Town	18,450	1–1	1		2	3	4	5	6	7	8	9	10		11
Replay	10/1/62	A	Luton Town	23,818	1–1	1		2	3	4	5	6	7	8	9	10		11
2nd Replay	15/1/62	N	Luton Town	29,438	5–1	1		2	3	4	5	6	7	8	9	10	11	
3rd Round	28/1/62	A	Norwich City	39,890	1–1	1	2	3	4	5	6	7	8	9	10	11		
Replay	31/1/62	H	Norwich City	29,796	1–2	1	2	3	4	5	6	7	8	9	10	11		

Friendlies

	Date	Venue	Opponents	Attendance	Score	Roy Bailey	Carberry	Compton	Baxter	Nelson	Thrower	Elsworthy	Laurel	Pickett	Stephenson	Moran	Crawford	Phillips	Leadbetter
Floodlights	9/10/61	A	Kettering Town	5,500	5–1	1	2	3	4		5		6		7	8	9	10	11
Haig Fund	6/11/61	A	Cambridge City	5,500	3–2	1	2	3		5	4	6			7	8	9	10	11
Friendly	17/2/62	H	TSV Alemannia Aachen	10,765	5–0	1	2	3	4	5				6	7	8	9	10	11

Table of all Division One Results, 1961/62

	Arsenal	Aston Villa	Birmingham City	Blackburn Rovers	Blackpool	Bolton Wanderers	Burnley	Cardiff City	Chelsea	Everton	Fulham	Ipswich Town	Leicester City	Manchester City	Manchester United	Nottingham Forest	Sheffield United	Sheffield Wednesday	Tottenham Hotspur	West Bromwich Albion	West Ham United	Wolverhampton Wanderers
Arsenal		4–5	1–1	0–0	3–0	1–2	2–2	1–1	0–3	2–3	1–0	0–3	4–4	3–0	5–1	2–1	2–0	1–0	2–1	0–1	2–2	3–1
Aston Villa	3–1		1–3	1–0	5–0	3–0	0–2	2–2	3–1	1–1	2–0	3–0	8–3	2–1	1–1	5–1	0–0	1–0	0–0	1–0	2–4	1–0
Birmingham City	1–0	0–2		2–1	1–1	2–1	2–6	3–0	3–2	0–0	2–1	3–1	1–5	1–1	1–1	1–1	3–0	1–1	2–3	1–2	4–0	3–6
Blackburn Rovers	0–0	4–2	2–0		1–1	2–3	2–1	0–0	3–0	1–1	0–2	2–2	2–1	4–1	3–0	2–1	1–2	0–2	0–1	1–1	1–0	2–1
Blackpool	0–1	1–2	1–0	2–1		2–1	1–3	0–4	0–1	1–2	1–1	1–2	2–1	3–1	2–3	1–3	2–4	1–3	1–2	2–2	2–0	7–2
Bolton Wanderers	2–1	1–1	3–2	1–1	0–0		0–0	1–1	4–2	1–1	2–3	0–0	1–0	0–2	1–0	6–1	2–0	4–3	1–2	3–2	1–0	1–0
Burnley	0–2	3–0	7–1	0–1	2–0	3–1		2–1	1–1	2–1	2–1	4–3	2–0	6–3	1–3	0–0	4–2	4–0	2–2	3–1	6–0	3–3
Cardiff City	1–1	1–0	3–2	1–1	3–2	1–2	1–1		5–2	0–0	0–3	0–3	0–4	0–0	1–2	2–2	1–1	2–1	1–1	2–2	3–0	2–3
Chelsea	2–3	1–0	1–1	1–1	1–0	1–0	1–2	2–3		1–1	0–0	2–2	1–3	1–1	2–0	2–2	6–1	1–0	0–2	4–1	0–1	4–5
Everton	4–1	2–0	4–1	1–0	2–1	1–0	2–2	8–3	4–0		3–0	5–2	3–2	0–2	5–1	6–0	1–0	0–4	3–0	3–1	3–0	4–0
Fulham	5–2	3–1	0–1	2–0	0–1	2–2	3–5	0–1	3–4	2–1		1–2	2–1	3–4	2–0	1–1	5–2	0–2	1–1	1–2	2–0	0–1
Ipswich Town	2–2	2–0	4–1	2–1	1–1	2–1	6–2	1–0	5–2	4–2	2–4		1–0	2–4	4–1	1–0	4–0	2–1	3–2	3–0	4–2	3–2
Leicester City	0–1	0–2	1–2	2–0	0–2	1–1	2–6	3–0	2–0	2–0	4–1	0–2		2–0	4–3	2–1	4–1	1–0	2–3	1–0	2–2	3–0
Manchester City	3–2	1–0	1–4	3–1	2–4	2–1	1–1	3–2	2–1	3–0	3–1	0–2	3–1		6–3	0–1	1–1	1–0	4–1	1–1	2–0	0–2
Manchester United	2–3	2–0	0–0	2–6	0–1	0–3	1–4	3–0	1–4	1–1	3–0	5–0	2–2	3–2		6–3	0–1	1–1	1–0	4–1	1–1	2–0
Nottingham Forest	0–1	2–0	2–1	1–2	3–4	0–1	3–2	2–1	3–0	2–1	1–1	1–1	0–0	1–2	1–0		2–0	3–1	2–0	4–4	3–0	3–1
Sheffield United	2–1	0–2	3–1	0–0	2–1	3–1	2–0	1–0	3–2	2–1	3–1	2–3	2–0	1–0	1–1	1–1		1–0	1–1	1–1	1–4	2–1
Sheffield Wednesday	1–1	3–0	5–1	1–0	3–2	4–2	4–0	2–0	5–3	2–1	1–1	1–4	1–2	1–0	3–1	3–0	1–2		0–0	2–1	0–0	3–2
Tottenham Hotspur	4–3	1–0	3–1	4–1	5–2	2–2	4–2	3–2	5–2	3–1	4–2	1–3	1–2	2–0	2–2	4–2	3–3	4–0		1–2	2–2	1–0
West Bromwich Albion	4–0	1–1	0–0	4–0	7–1	6–2	1–1	5–1	4–0	2–0	2–0	1–3	2–0	2–2	1–1	2–2	3–1	0–2	2–4		0–1	1–1
West Ham United	3–3	2–0	2–2	2–3	2–2	1–0	2–1	4–1	2–1	3–1	4–2	2–2	4–1	0–4	1–1	3–2	1–2	2–3	2–1	3–3		4–2
Wolverhampton Wanderers	2–3	2–2	2–1	0–2	2–2	5–1	1–1	1–1	1–1	0–3	1–3	2–0	1–1	4–1	2–2	2–1	0–1	3–0	3–1	1–5	3–2	

Bibliography

Books

Armfield, Jimmy (ed.), *All Star Football Book No. 2*, Souvenir Press Ltd, 1962

Bowler, Dave, *Winning Isn't Everything: A Biography of Sir Alf Ramsey*, Gollancz, 1998

Butler, Frank and Gunn, Malcolm (eds), *News of the World Football Annual 1962/63*, News of the World, 1962

Dimmock, Peter (ed.), *BBC TV Sportsview Bookof Soccer 1962*, Vernon Holdings, 1962

Eastwood, John and Moyse, Tony, *The Men Who Made the Town*, Almeida Books, 1986

Fabian, A.H. & Prole, R.W. (eds), *Caxton Football Yearbook: 1962*, Caxton Publishing, 1962

FA Yearbook 1962/63, Naldrett Press, 1962

Greaves, Jimmy and Giller, Norman *The Sixties Revisited*, Queen Anne Press, 1992

Hadgraft, Rob, *Ipswich Town Champions of England*, Desert Island Books, 2002

Hill, Jimmy, *Striking for Soccer*, The Sportsmans Book Club, 1963

Hopcraft, Arthur, *The Football Man*, Collins, 1968

Lord, Bob, *My Fight for Football*, S. Paul, 1963

Marquis, Max, *Anatomy of a Football Manager*, Arthur Baker, 1970

Moyse, Tony, *Suffolk Punch, Ipswich Town 1936–96*, Extra Cover, 1996

Peskett, Roy, *Daily Mail Guide To Football 1962/63*, Associated Newspapers, 1962

Rollin, Jack, *World Soccer Digest 1962/63*, Echo Publications (London) Ltd, 1962

The World Book of Football Champions, Purnell & Sons, 1962

Topical Times Football Book 1962/63, D.C. Thomson, 1962

Newspapers

Daily Express
Daily Herald
Daily Telegraph
East Anglian Daily Times
Evening Star
Observer
The Times